MID-GEORGIAN BRITAIN

1740–69

Jacqueline Riding

SHIRE LIVING HISTORIES

How we worked • How we played • How we lived

Published in Great Britain in 2010 by Shire Publications Ltd,
Midland House, West Way, Botley, Oxford OX2 0PH,
United Kingdom.
44-02 23rd Street, Suite 219, Long Island City, NY 11101,
USA.

E-mail: shire@shirebooks.co.uk   www.shirebooks.co.uk

© 2010 Shire Publications.

Every attempt has been made by the Publishers to secure
the appropriate permissions for materials reproduced in
this book. If there has been any oversight we will be happy
to rectify the situation and a written submission should be
made to the Publishers.

A CIP catalogue record for this book is available from the
British Library.

Shire Living Histories no. 7. ISBN-13: 978 0 74780 799 5

Jacqueline Riding has asserted her right under the
Copyright, Designs and Patents Act, 1988, to be identified
as the author of this book.

Designed by Myriam Bell Design, France and typeset in
Perpetua, Janson Text and Gill Sans.

Printed in China through Worldprint Ltd.

10 11 12 13 14   10 9 8 7 6 5 4 3 2 1

ACKNOWLEDGEMENTS

Bridgeman Art Library: Bibliotheque Nationale, Paris,
pages 4, 33 (top), Felbrigg Hall, The National Trust page
52 (bottom), Fitzwilliam Museum, Cambridge, pages 16
(top), 21, 32 (bottom), The Foundling Museum, pages 13,
35 (bottom), 66, 70, 71, Guildhall Library, City of
London, pages 12, 43, 69, Harewood House Trust, page 32
(top), Lobkowicz Palace, Prague Castle page 53, Louvre,
Paris, page 14, Museum of London, page 36, The National
Army Museum, page 68 (top), National Gallery of
Victoria, Melbourne, page 16 (bottom), The National
Gallery, London, pages 17, 20, 31, 68 (bottom), The
National Museums Liverpool, page 64 (top), Norwich
Castle Museum & Art Gallery, page 72, Nottingham City
Museums & Galleries, page 44, Private collections, pages
52 (top), 55, 60, 64 (bottom), Sir John Soane's Museum,
page 11, Victoria & Albert Museum, London, pages 30, 48
(top), Victoria Art Gallery, Bath, pages 46 (bottom), 65
(bottom), Wolverhampton Art Gallery, page 46 (top), Yale
Center for British Art, cover and pages 19, 33 (bottom),
42 (bottom), 48 (bottom), 50; British Library, pages 6, 10
(top), 38 (top), 40, 49, 61, 63, 65 (top), 76, 77 (top);
Compton Verney, Warwickshire, pages 58, 62;
Dr Johnson's House, pages 8 (top), 9, 10 (bottom); Fairfax
House, York Civic Trust, page 26 (bottom); Handel House
Collections Trust, pages 8 (bottom), 22, 27; The House of
St Barnabas, pages 25 (bottom) and 26 (top); The Royal
College of Surgeons of England, pages 18 (top and
bottom), 29, 74 (top and bottom), 75 (top and bottom),
77 (bottom); Shire Publications, by Nick Hardcastle,
pages 56–7.

All other images supplied by the author.

COVER IMAGE
This small group portrait, known as a 'conversation',
depicts an aristocratic London townhouse complete with
high ceiling, panelled 'wainscot' walls, green silk damask
hangings, an enormous 'Turkey' rug and large
landscape/still-life paintings in gilded frames. The
assembled family and friends of the diplomat and
politician, Lord Harrington, play cards and drink tea.

Shire Publications is supporting the Woodland Trust, the UK's leading woodland conservation charity, by funding the dedication of trees.

CONTENTS

PREFACE

THE CENTRAL DECADES of the eighteenth century, before the Industrial Revolution shifted power and people to the cities of the north, saw the capital city London take an overwhelmingly preponderant place in the social, economic, political and cultural life of the nation. Indeed, it could claim a place in the life of Europe itself, as, even if Paris could claim a more refined society, Vienna to be more vibrant artistically, or Rome to be more spiritually powerful, London was the largest city of Europe, and surely by a large margin the most rumbustuous. It was a place of larger-than-life personalities with great energy, a place where no-one did anything by halves. In its streets, men and women of every rank rubbed shoulders and made fortunes; few were happy to be away for long, and most of those who lived elsewhere looked for ways to get themselves to the capital. Despite the poverty, squalor and heartbreak that Hogarth in particular portrayed with such clarity, in these years, life in London was life in Britain.

Life in mid-eighteenth-century London is portrayed for us amazingly vividly by its artists, writers, novelists and diarists; Hogarth and Samuel Johnson pre-eminent among them but Fielding and many others not far behind. Its confidence was epitomized by the splendours of the German George Frideric Handel who made this his home and whose music resounds today. Jacqueline Riding, an expert on eighteenth-century history and culture, recreates his world. It is one that maintains a perennial hold on the British imagination today.

Peter Furtado
General Editor

William Hogarth, *Gin Lane*, 1751. Depicting the poverty-stricken area of St Giles, London, a sculpture of King George II can be seen at a safe distance, atop the spire of St George's Church, Bloomsbury.

INTRODUCTION: LONDON AND LIFE

I suggested a doubt, that were I to reside in London, the exquisite zest with which I relished it in occasional visits might go off, and I might grow tired of it. JOHNSON. 'Why, Sir, you find no man, at all intellectual, who is willing to leave London. No, Sir, when a man is tired of London, he is tired of life; for there is in London all that life can afford.

Samuel Johnson's legendary comment to James Boswell in 1777 hints at a city of dramatic contrasts, variety and reinvention, capable of entertaining and stimulating the most voracious appetite. Johnson clearly revelled in the opportunities and novelties that this world city provided and was drawn to the energy and glamour of a population on the make and on the up. After all, forty years previously and in the company of the actor David Garrick, he had walked from his native Lichfield to the capital (118 miles as the crow flies) with barely the clothes he stood up in. The population of London and the parameters of the city expanded dramatically over the century, so much so that contemporary observers were unsure of the number of dwellings, let alone the souls that occupied them. According to *The history and survey of the Cities of London and Westminster, Borough of Southwark, and parts adjacent* of 1753, London extended from Limehouse in the east to Tothill Street, Westminster in the west (calculated as 7½ miles) and from St. Leonard's, Shoreditch in the north to the furthest end of Blackman-Street in Southwark to the south (2½ miles). By 1770, the revised *Survey* could declare, 'A modern author, speaking of London, says, "This Ancient City has ingulphed one City, one Borough, and forty-two villages..." to which number we may now fairly add Paddington, and Marybone'. The author concludes with the prophetic statement:

Opposite: Richard Parr after John Roque, *An exact survey of the Cities of London, Westminster, & Borough of Southwark...* 1745–6.

...nor is it at all unlikely, if the modern rage of building continues, that London will become one immense line of houses from Epping Forest

James Watson
after Joshua
Reynolds, *Dr
Samuel Johnson*,
1770.

to Hounslow Heath; since, even at present, little more is necessary to make it so, than some houses of communication between Hounslow and Brentford, and the same between Stratford and the edge of the Forest.

Within the same sources, the population of London was estimated as being 767,176 in 1738, 992,000 in 1746 growing to 1,200,000 by 1770, calculated from an estimated 95,897 (1738), 124,000 (1746) and 150,000 (1770) dwellings with an average of eight persons living in each. Regardless of the actual figures (currently estimated as 650,000 mid-century and over ten per cent of the population of England) they were right on one essential point: London was big. It was by far the largest city in Europe, and since the formation of the new political entity of Great Britain (by the Act of Union in 1707), the British centre of Court and politics, trade and commerce, wealth, entertainment and consumption. Countless commentators could vouch that all human life and activity existed there, good and bad. In our own time the novelist Jamila Gavin, author of *Coram Boy* (2000), has likened the London of the mid-eighteenth century to modern-day Kolkata. To grasp the sensory onslaught of a stroll around mid-eighteenth century London and the visible diversity in appearance and wealth of its

Unknown
engraver, *A View of
St George's Church
Hanover Square*,
1751. Designed
by John James and
consecrated in
1725, this was
George Frideric
Handel's parish
church.

neighbourhoods and citizens, we must put aside all preconceptions of the 'Age of Elegance' or at the very least allow that for every Hanover Square or Handel's *Messiah*, there was a 'Gin Lane' and Gay's *The Beggar's Opera*.

The London journal of Dr Johnson's friend and biographer, James Boswell (written in 1762–3) notoriously details how a man of leisure, on a reasonable allowance, could occupy his time from sunrise to sunset and beyond. Relatively few were as idle – that is, without employment – nor as pleasure-seeking and predatory as Boswell, yet the public arena, in all its diversity, was essentially designed as male rather than female territory. In the main, women, whether wives or whores, serviced and supported this male world. But with such opportunity and 'freedom' came responsibility. With few respectable trades or occupations open to them, a majority of women, with a few noble and ignoble exceptions, relied on their menfolk for income and status, and therefore a family's security rose and fell with the success and failure of its male head of household.

Even a figure as well-connected and ingenious as Dr Johnson found himself at times unable to afford lodgings – success was precarious as were the accompanying trappings of even a modestly comfortable lifestyle. The relentless proximity for many Londoners to poverty and disaster was an accepted fact, to be battled against and defeated by fair means or foul. Bankruptcy lists, published daily in London newspapers, and overpopulated debtors' prisons (the Fleet was the most notorious), indicate this constant and almost universal struggle for survival, in an age where support from state or parish was effectively non-existent. The accepted role of national government was to maintain law and order at home and fight the enemy abroad. The dismal progresses of William Hogarth's 'Rake' and 'Harlot', circulated throughout the population via the artist's own exclusive prints and then cheap 'pirated' reproductions, may have been extreme examples of life and death in a disinterested, unforgiving urban environment, but to many they were cautionary tales, tracing the complexity, hardship and even fragility of contemporary life.

Exterior of Dr Johnson's House, Gough Square, City of London. Built in 1700 and Johnson's home 1748–59. His famous dictionary (1755) was compiled in the garret.

G. F. Handel, 'Hallelujah Chorus' from *Messiah*, autograph score, 1741.

Not all was doom and gloom. There was theatre, opera, art, pleasure gardens and literature. This was the age of Handel, Garrick, Fielding, Hogarth and Gainsborough, the English oratorio and the first public art exhibitions. And there was civic as well as domestic love and kindness, honour and integrity. Religion still held a place in everyday life – this was also the age of John Wesley and evangelical 'Methodism' (see page 68) and if all was well with you and yours, it was expected that the prosperous citizen and good Christian should seek out and help those who could not help themselves. Such a citizen need not look far. For wealth and poverty sat cheek by jowl, even in the most affluent and fashionable districts. Lincoln's Inn Fields, an elegant seventeenth-century development still desirable to the upwardly mobile in the mid-eighteenth century, was located within yards of the notorious haunts of the Holborn gangs and street criminals. On the monthly execution day a Mayfair resident, ambling to his new brick town house off Grosvenor Square, would have to push his way through the boisterous, that is drunken, crowds thronging the streets and side-

The first floor of Dr Johnson's House, Gough Square. The white partition panelling used to subdivide the first floor has been pushed back to cover the stairwell (centre). Doors set within it allow access to and from the stairs.

William Hogarth, 'Scene VIII: The Rake in Bedlam' from *A Rake's Progress*, 1734. His fortune spent, body ravaged and wits irretrievably lost, the Rake's progress terminates in London's notorious lunatic asylum.

alleys to Tyburn's 'Hanging Tree' just north of his house, avoiding the inevitable hordes of prostitutes, muggers and pickpockets. However as a propertied and therefore voting male, one of the small percentage of men enfranchised at this time, he would have had greater recourse to justice than most of those who faced the full brunt of the English penal system. The law was, almost without exception, on the side of the propertied and wealthy. Sentences for relatively minor thefts were severe, pillorying, hangings and deportations standard: there was no custodial sentencing.

But the criminal and the respectable were closer still than most would care to admit. The historian Dan Cruickshank has argued that whole areas of Georgian London were built on the extraordinary earnings of a diverse, all-pervading and conspicuous sex-trade. And as the century advanced, and trade and the nascent empire expanded, Britain's and therefore London's wealth would be inextricably linked with another kind of human trade. Any discussion on Georgian luxury goods must be prefaced with human exploitation in general and the transatlantic slave trade in particular. It has been estimated that as much as half of Britain's wealth derived directly or indirectly from the trade.

Many things divided Georgian opinion, politics for one. In 1740, the country had been for almost twenty years under the pragmatic, some would say unprincipled, leadership of Sir Robert Walpole. On his resignation in 1742, the Whigs continued to lead the government throughout the period until the reign of George III (r. 1760–1820)

William Hogarth, 'Plate XI: The Idle 'Prentice Executed at Tyburn' from *Industry and Idleness*, 1747. Unlike his fellow apprentice, who through industry has become Lord Mayor of London, the Idle Apprentice pays the ultimate price for his degenerate and ultimately worthless life.

who had Tory leanings and the William Pitts, Elder and Younger. But if anything could unite Britons, it was the French. True Britons saw their independence and freedom as in marked contrast to their French cousins who, whether they realised it or not, struggled under the yoke of an absolute, tyrannical and bellicose monarchy. Throughout this period, indeed for more or less the whole of the eighteenth century, Britain was at war with France, whether on mainland Europe, in the American colonies or the Indian subcontinent. This ongoing struggle with the 'old enemy' abroad would in turn fuel unrest and rebellion at home. The Jacobite cause of the exiled James II/VII and his male heirs, removed from the thrones of England, Scotland and Ireland after the Glorious Revolution of 1688, gained renewed impetus with the arrival of a new British Royal dynasty, the House of Hanover (1714). Jacobite uprisings in support of James VIII (the Old Pretender) and his son Charles Edward (the Young Pretender) had occurred with regularity and with French support throughout the reign of George I (r.1714–27) but erupted in 1745–6 during the reign of his son George II (r.1727–60) into what was arguably the greatest home-grown threat faced by the Hanoverians and the ruling Whig party. The Seven Years' War (1756–63) and American War of Independence (1775–83) were further examples of the global nature of British–French rivalry.

In 1709, the journalist and author Daniel Defoe set out the key English economic groups as:

1. The great, who live profusely.
2. The rich, who live plentifully.
3. The middle sort, who live well.

4. The working trades, who labour hard, but feel no want.

5. The country people, farmers, &c, who fare indifferently.

6. The poor, that fare hard.

7. The miserable, that really pinch and suffer want.

Defining a cohesive 'middle class' is problematic – then as now – but essentially the present volume looks at the lives of those in Defoe's third group, with the lower end of the second and the upper end of the fourth. The gradual but conscious expansion of Defoe's 'middling sort' into the level above is a significant social shift of the eighteenth century. This was the threshold of the Industrial Revolution, with all the economic and social changes to the rural and urban environment that this would bring. Contemporary observers noted the apparent ease by which gentility could be acquired via this expanding prosperity, and thus how new blood from trade or the professions swelled the ranks of the 'genteel'.

Before proceeding, a caveat is necessary. This study is inevitably partial and selective. A great many things through necessity have been omitted. But, like London itself, contrast and variety are the essence.

William Hogarth, *The March of the Guards to Finchley*, 1749–50. At the Tottenham Court Road Turnpike, British soldiers indulge in some last-minute revelry before marching north against the advancing Jacobite Army.

LOVE AND SEX, MARRIAGE AND FAMILY

A KEY ACTIVITY of any man, and *the* key activity of any woman, was to marry and have children. A woman was expected to be a virgin on her wedding night. The 1740s saw a spate of louche memoirs and novels, such as John Cleland's fictional *Memoirs of a Woman of Pleasure* ('Fanny Hill', 1748–9) and the salacious reminiscences of the courtesan Constantia Phillips (1748) in which she declared her career in prostitution was the result of being raped at the age of twelve by an unnamed aristocrat. These were countered by 'conduct' books aimed at the middling sort, which stated with mantra-like regularity, that a woman's modesty and good reputation were her most valued possessions. A stated aim of Samuel Richardson's *Pamela: or, virtue rewarded* (1740–2), the literary sensation of the decade, was 'to give practical Examples, worthy to be followed in the most critical and affecting Cases, by the modest Virgin, the chaste Bride, and the obliging Wife.' Describing the successful defence of the heroine's chastity and her 'reward', that is marriage with her reformed aggressor, it was effectively a conduct book, cunningly disguised as a novel. Men who debauched and abandoned unmarried virgins were below contempt firstly, for removing a chaste female from the marriage market (of whatever segment of society) and secondly, as in the case of Constantia Phillips, for setting in train a tragic descent into vice and prostitution.

Prostitution was considered not only immoral, but a conduit for disease between individuals, and worse still, spouses and offspring. It therefore affected (or infected) the very security and future of the family. This fear was illustrated by Hogarth in his *Marriage A-la-Mode* series: the syphilis contracted during the husband's philandering finds ultimate expression in the deformed limb of his only, and probably sterile, offspring. Condoms made of linen or animal bladder/intestine were available from barbers and taverns. Wearing this reusable prophylactic was described by Boswell as being 'in armour'.

Opposite: Thomas Gainsborough, *Conversation in a Park*, portrait of the artist and his wife, Margaret Burr at the time of their marriage, 1746. Aged eighteen and nineteen respectively, the couple's marriage lasted despite Gainsborough's philandering and a bout of the clap.

Joseph Highmore, 'Scene XII: Pamela tells a nursery tale' from *Twelve Scenes from Richardson's Pamela*, 1743–4. Pamela's reward is a loving marriage and contented motherhood (which includes caring for her husband's illegitimate daughter). Richardson states that she is a flexible follower of John Locke.

Such items no doubt assisted but ultimately did not stem the tide of sexually transmitted diseases and unwanted pregnancies (see page 69–70). Some commentators advocated marriage not only for health reasons but for sexual pleasure, as argued by the author of *Friendly Advice* (1763): 'For there can be no true Pleasure without Affection; no real Enjoyment without Love. Unlawful Intercourse is Lust, and can never meet with the Satisfaction it wants.'

Joseph Highmore, 'Scene III: Pamela Fainting' from *Twelve Scenes from Richardson's Pamela*, 1743–4. Mr B (the virgin Pamela's guardian) attempts to rape her.

For many therefore, sex only within marriage was essential and for very good reason. Despite a family's desire for a sizeable cash injection or (preferably and) increased status deriving from the judicious marriage of a son, daughter or sibling, there is a sense that love and mutual respect, although not essential, were at least preferable. Whether experience came anywhere near this ideal is debatable: disastrous marriages clearly existed, as suggested by Dr Johnson's world-weary comment, that 'a second marriage is the triumph of hope over experience'. Yet some women clearly desired more than mere contentment and security and would go to great lengths to get it:

William Hogarth, 'Scene VI: The Lady's Death' from *Marriage A-la-Mode*, 1745. Her lover hanged for the murder of her feckless husband, the countess expires from poison, caressed by her diseased child.

A young lady who, when of age, will have a fortune of 20,000 l. [pounds] eloped with a clergyman, who, it is supposed, has carried her to Scotland. Her guardian received a letter from her next morning, in which are these words, *Love has the wings of a dove, and I shall be gone too far to be overtaken.*

The *Gentleman's Magazine* (January 1764) was in no doubt as to the young lady's appeal to the unnamed cleric. This would come as no surprise to one Eobald Toze, who wrote in *The present state of Europe* of 1770 that the English, 'are extremely violent in their passions. And this in love no less than hatred; for certainly it is to the violence of the former passion, or avarice, that must be imputed the many unequal, and sometimes indecent marriages seen in England.'

Bearing in mind the vagaries of contemporary life, money really did matter. Further, as society in general did not favour divorce (a process almost impossible for women to instigate), marrying in haste to repent at leisure was a very real prospect. Marriage announcements tended to focus on how much the woman was worth, sometimes her looks, and little else. For example, the second marriage of Daniel Twining to Mary or Molly Little, the daughter of a Peterborough merchant, is described in the *London Evening Post* (6 February 1746) as follows: 'On Thursday last was married, at Somerset House chapel, Mr. Twining, an eminent

Syphilitic skull from John Hunter's Collection.

Tea-man in the Strand, to Miss Molly Little, of Peterborough in Northamptonshire, a beautiful young Lady, with a Fortune of 8000 l.' The full potential of this marriage was actually realized five years later, as this advertisement in the same newspaper (4 Feb 1751) regarding a forthcoming auction in Peterborough reveals: 'Divers Freehold, Copyhold, and Leasehold Estates...late the Estate of Richard Little, Esq; For Particulars thereof enquire of Mr. Roger Pinckney at Peterborough aforesaid, or Mr. Twining in Devereux-Court, Temple-Bar, London.' Canny Mr Twining.

The onus for domestic felicity was very much the responsibility of the wife, at least as espoused in treatises by male authors, Thomas Marriott's *Female Conduct: being an Essay on the Art of Pleasing. To be practised by the Fair Sex, before and after marriage* (London, 1759) and William Kenrick's *The Whole Duty of Woman* (London, 1753) to name but two. Set out in crypto-biblical language and structure, the latter offers a point-by-point guide to conjugal happiness:

> Love him as the partner of thy happiness, as the sharer of the pleasures and pains of mortality. Without love the husband is a tyrant, and the woman is a slave. The matrimonial vow is a commercial contract without affection; 'tis the shadow of marriage, and not the substance thereof.
>
> Neglect not the little arts of endearment; but let the charm, which captivated the lover, secure the attachment of the husband. Forget not the elegance of thy virginity, but appear every morning as at the morning of the bridal day.

Condom, caecal membrane and silk, 1790–1810. Available new in various fabrics and substances (and therefore price ranges), condoms were also cleaned and sold second-hand.

Excellent advice no doubt, but it does seem a little one-sided. However, simply because these conduct books existed does not mean necessarily that women bought them, or even read them. It is certainly an indication of the writer's attitude towards women and marriage, or perhaps even wishful thinking on the part of the male purchaser. But generally speaking, marriage and family were perceived as microcosms of the body politic and nation. The apportioning of power and duties, hierarchies and loyalties required to maintain a peaceful and contented nation correlated to those required for a successful marriage, as Kenrick continues:

Be thou obedient, for the law of superiority is given to man from above, and subjection is the portion of the daughters of Eve... As rebellion lifteth up its head against its sovereign, and thereby adds weight to the yoak it attempted to shake off; so the subjection of a wife, when she usurpeth to govern, should be converted into servitude.

Yet Eobald Toze stated that in England, 'The husbands are generally so indulgent to their wives, that they are looked upon to be the happiest in the world'. Regardless of emotional binds, the law, as Kenrick's quotes above suggest, was on the side of the husband and, except in very particular circumstances, the wife and all her possessions transferred to his ownership on marriage.

Once joined, the social and familial pressure to fulfil the primary purpose of marriage must have been immense. Personal inclination and desire for children aside, legitimate children provided continuity of family and estate, no matter how small the inheritance. Blood ties were powerful and there was every expectation of one or other of the children caring for their parents in later life. Numerous advertisements offering cures for impotency and infertility hint at the misery and desperation of childlessness. The *General Advertiser* (11 August 1752) advertised,

William Hogarth, a scene from *The Beggar's Opera*, 1729. The actress Lavinia Fenton, kneeling (right), faces her then lover the Duke of Bolton (far right). Eobald Toze may have had their 'unequal' marriage (1751) in mind (see page 17).

'The True Cordial Quintessence of the Vipers … for the real, substantial Cure of Impotence in Men, and Barrenness in Women.' This concoction professed to not only,

William Hogarth, *The Graham Children*, 1742. The painting contains allusions to vulnerability, the cat eyeing the caged bird, top right, and mortality, the cherub with scythe located above Thomas's head.

furnish Matter, and create Desire, but also true Power (as it braces up and corroborates the Testes) and gives an elastick Springiness to the Musculi Erectores Penis in Men, and corrects, cleanses, and comforts the Uterus, or Womb in Women, the Lankness and Luxity of the former, and the Foulness, Coldness, or Obstruction of the latter, being more the Cause of Impotency or Infertility, in the one Sex, and Indifferency or Stirility in the other, than any Thing else beside.

Achieving pregnancy, as we know, was the beginning rather than the end. Childbirth, although a highly desirable, everyday event, was in

many cases dangerous, and in some fatal. In a letter to the Editor of the *Gentleman's Magazine* (1750) one woman observed:

> I have been the mother of eleven children, and have had exceeding hard labours with them all, and should be glad to know of the Doctor, or some other wise gentleman, why my creator appointed the primary end of my creation, to be attended with such unutterable pain and sorrow. Your, &c. MATERNA.

For a 'speedy Delivery when the Throws are great', Eliza Smith in *The Compleat Housewife* (11th edition, 1742) recommended taking 'half a dram of borax powdered, and mixed with a glass of white-wine, some sugar, and a little cinnamon-water: if it does no good the first time, try it again two hours after; so likewise the third time.'

Although historians have perceived a sea-change in attitudes to children and childhood during this period – the first full-length novel for children, Sarah Fielding's *The Governess* was published in 1749 – it was still the case that children were not simply children, but future citizens. The most influential book on education in the eighteenth century was John Locke's *Some thoughts concerning education*, first published in 1690. In the 'Epistle Dedicatory' Locke writes, 'The well Educating of their Children is so much the Duty and Concern of Parents, and the Welfare and Prosperity of the Nation so much depends on it, that I would have every one lay it seriously to Heart'. 'Diversions' and play 'should be directed towards good useful Habits, or else they will introduce ill ones.' Exercise was highly recommended.

Child mortality was very high, even in wealthier families. In urban environments between one-fifth and a quarter of live births died before the age of two. Hogarth's *The Graham Children* (1742), a beautiful evocation of contented childhood amongst the wealthier middling sort, also contains a tragic reminder of its fragility and transience. The infant, Thomas, died before the portrait was completed.

William Hogarth, *After* from 'Before and After', oil on canvas, c. 1730–1. The elegant, balletic courtship of *Before* has descended into flushed and dishevelled bewilderment.

21

HOME AND
NEIGHBOURHOOD

THE CITY OF LONDON maintained its medieval street plan after the Great Fire of 1666 and was therefore a densely populated area of narrow winding streets and alleys. In contrast the new developments in the west and east ends from the late seventeenth century onwards tended towards a formal grid format, often punctuated by squares such as Hanover, Bloomsbury, Cavendish, St James's and Berkeley, which offered an attractive vista from the encircling houses and a pleasant space for promenading or simply passing through. John Roque's map of 1746 (page 6) illustrates this contrast in town planning between the City and the west and east ends. Key 'middling' areas could be found adjacent to new aristocratic developments, the streets off Grosvenor and Berkeley squares in Mayfair for example or in areas vacated by the aristocracy such as Lincoln's Inn Fields or Leicester Fields, where Hogarth, Sir Joshua Reynolds and later the surgeon John Hunter (younger brother of William, see page 77) lived. Apart from the palatial residences of the aristocracy – for example Northumberland House at Charing Cross (see page 52), Burlington House on the north side of Piccadilly – London streets were occupied by rows of brick terraced housing, with narrow street frontages and party walls, often created piecemeal in tight spaces by speculative builders who leased these plots from wealthy landowners. For this reason, unlike their contemporaries in most major European cities, Londoners lived vertically (i.e. on a series of connected floors) rather than horizontally in 'apartments'. Aside from the freestanding great houses of the aristocracy, all London houses from artisan upwards were a form of terraced house.

The composer George Frideric Handel (1685–1759), a British citizen from 1727, lived in London for fifty years and in one particular house in Mayfair, now No. 25 Brook Street, for thirty-six of those years. This house was built in the 1720s of an average size and type that continued to be attractive to the aspirational middling sort. Further, as

Opposite: John Buckler, *Handel's House*, 1839. Handel is whimsically depicted peering out from the principal entertaining room (probably used for rehearsing). Beyond the railings can be seen the tops of the basement kitchen windows.

Houses on Fournier (originally Church) Street, Spitalfields, built in the second quarter of the eighteenth century.

stated above, the building restrictions within London meant that aside from subtle variation or detailing, houses tended to follow this familiar format. Benjamin Franklin for example lodged from 1757–75 within a similar house built in the 1730s on Craven Street (now No. 36) near Charing Cross. Meard Street and Broad Street (now Broadwick Street)

The front room on the first floor, No. 36 Craven Street, Westminster. (Benjamin Franklin House.) Franklin's lodgings consisted of three rooms on the first floor. The 'raised and fielded' panelling and shutters are painted 'warm stone'.

in Soho still have excellent examples from the 1720 and 1730s and perhaps the most complete and therefore evocative series of streets from this period are found to the north of Christ Church in Spitalfields.

Handel was in the middle of the 'middling sort', not quite comfortable enough to stop working, if he had wanted to of course, nor indeed a 'lowly' tradesman. His house and contents therefore were not ostentatious, nor overly fashionable. It was a serviceable, respectable dwelling. He lived alone, although the house could have accommodated a family, with at least two, possibly three servants. Unlike the other servants whose quarters were in the garrets on the third floor, the cook lived out. Room use was flexible, although conventions did exist. Both Franklin's and Handel's house had two main rooms on each of the main floors – basement (kitchens), ground (parlours), first (formal dining/entertainment) and second (best bedroom/dressing room) – with a small closet room at the rear, on the ground to second floors. Closets were a standard although not universal feature and had a door, window and perhaps a stove. Comfortable and private spaces that warmed up quickly in the winter months, Franklin used his as a bedroom.

The front doors in both houses led into a passage, ending in a dog-leg staircase at the rear which connected every floor, including

Above: Looking into the stairwell, left, and back room, right (Franklin's laboratory), from the front room, first floor, No. 36 Craven Street, Westminster. (Benjamin Franklin House.) To the left of the marble corner fire surround is another door that leads to the closet or 'powder room' where Franklin slept.

Left: Exterior of Richard Beckford's house, Soho Square. Built in 1746, the house remained a shell until Beckford's ownership from 1754. His brother William, Lord Mayor of London lived nearby at No. 22 Soho Square.

(via a door) the basement kitchen area. A space between the window and pavement at the front, a standard innovation in town houses, allowed light and air to enter the basement area, invaluable for a steamy kitchen. The entire interior above ground was panelled (wainscot) with pine or deal, and painted. This form of wall covering was gradually replaced by plaster, which was either painted or wallpapered. The new houses of wealthy merchants and tradesmen, at the very upper end of what could be described as 'middling', could be lavish in comparison. During the 1750s, Richard Beckford (City of London Alderman and MP for Bristol), whose family had accrued enormous wealth in Jamaica as planters and exporters of rum, sugar and molasses, commissioned ornate plasterwork interiors in a house on the south-east corner of Soho Square. The 1770s saw the dominance of the Adam brothers and their style, which they described as a 'beautiful variety of light mouldings, gracefully formed, delicately enriched and arranged with propriety and skill'. Their major London speculative development, the Adelphi (built 1768–72) was located between the Strand and the Thames, and was a sequence of

Above: The Drawing Room, Richard Beckford's house, Soho Square. The plaster ceiling design includes representations of the four seasons and elements (central medallion). The overmantel is original.

Left: Fairfax House, York, was created in 1762 to the designs of John Carr (see also Harewood House, page 32). The plasterwork on the Great Staircase is of the finest detail and quality, something only the aristocracy or the super-wealthy could afford.

twenty-four terraced houses in this new, domestic neoclassical style. It was a financial disaster, despite celebrity endorsement from David Garrick.

The early eighteenth-century paint colours or 'drabs', dark tones such as olive green and mid-grey (as seen in No. 25 Brook Street), had gradually given way to lighter stone colours (as seen at Franklin's house) through to pale blue, prior to the Adam polychromes. To avoid the disruption and expense of regular redecoration, a dark chocolate brown was applied to areas more susceptible to wear and tear such as skirtings, doors and door/window architraves (seen at Craven and Brook Street). Window seats built into the panelling under the window openings were a standard feature and all windows, on the three floors above ground, had internal shutters for security, warmth and in the summer months, shade. The flooring, including the staircase, was usually oak boards, originally limed (a disinfectant) which was removed with a hard brush and water and then waxed rather than varnished. The ceilings were of a lime-plaster painted a soft white to reflect the light from the windows and candles.

The staircase of No. 25 Brook Street, looking into the front room on the first floor.

The fact that No. 25 Brook Street was a single man's rented house no doubt affected the decoration and furnishing. Many people rented rather than owned (Franklin and Boswell are two other examples), but maintaining modish interiors was generally seen as the preserve of the mistress of the house. Handel's house was fashionable in the mid-1720s – in a rather restrained manner – but was decidedly old-fashioned by the time of his death in 1759. The simple paired curtains listed on all floors in the 1759 inventory had been replaced within fashionable circles since the 1730s by a single gathered piece of fabric that could be drawn up or down. 'Lincey' (coarse wool or cotton warp), 'Harrateen' (wool or wool/silk mix) and silk were still common bed, curtain and general upholstery fabrics as were the colours, white, cream, green and red. Blue was also popular. Bedlinens included sheets, bolster and pillows (linen), blankets (wool), a quilt (a thin wadding,

A section of the Adelphi (1768–72) on Adam Street (centre right), seen from John Adam Street.

sandwiched between ivory silk, which was then 'quilted' with running stitches forming a diaper or 'diamond' pattern) and a coverlet *en suite* with the bed furniture (or fabric) which in Handel's case was a crimson wool harrateen. The standard carpeting for the period was loose (rather than fitted) and invariably described as 'Turkey' rugs, denoting near-Eastern origin. Furniture and furnishings could be bought new, or in house sales. The following from the *General Advertiser* (22 January 1750) is a particularly lavish example but reveals what was available and considered attractive to potential customers:

> To be sold by Auction…at Mr Lambe's Great Auction Room Pallmall; A Large Parcel of rich household furniture, removed from the late Dwelling House of a Lady of QUALITY, deceas'd, (the House being lett;) consisting of rich Silk Damask, wrought Worsted Damask, Linnen and other Furnishings, good Bedding, Saffoys, French Elbow and other Chairs, covered in Crimson Silk Damask, rich Brocade, c. with Mahogany and Wallnutre carv'd Frames, curious India Japan and fine inlaid Italian Cabinets, Desks, Chests, and Screens, Library Cases with Looking-Glass Doors, noble, large

Sconces in rich French carv'd and gilt Frames, Turkey Carpets of various Sizes, Brussels Tapestry Hangings, Repeating Table, and other Clocks, a Harpsichord, two Iron Chests, some fine China, Furniture, Pictures, Fire-Arms, and other valuable Effects.

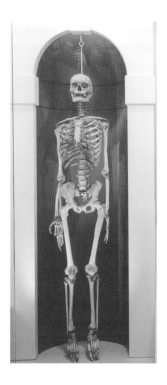

Note that the furniture includes walnut 'Wallnutre' and mahogany. Imported from central America, the latter was still an exotic novelty in the 1730s, but increasingly became the fashionable wood of choice. With such enticements, housebreaking or burglary was a hazard. In the Old Bailey proceedings of 23 February 1757, Gabriel Savoy was indicted for breaking and entering the home of William Moss and stealing items of silver, cutlery and clothing. The total value of the hoard was a matter of life and death:

> Q to prosecutrix. What is the value of these goods?
> Proseturix. The two table spoons cost 13 s. each, the six tea-spoons 18 s. the milkpot 30 s. the strainer half a crown.
> Q. Would the other things sell for 20 s.
> Prosecutor. I dare say they would and more.
> Guilty, Death.

The skeleton of Jonathan Wild, executed at Tyburn on 24 May 1725. Wild was the leader of a thieves' gang whilst masquerading as a 'thief-taker' or bounty hunter. He earned money by returning the goods his gang had stolen, occasionally turning in his own men for authenticity.

Finally, how closely did neighbours look out for each other? London's was a large, predominantly migrant population, who no doubt valued their privacy once the front door closed behind them. Yet, there seems to have been a general expectation that beyond family, someone somewhere would look out for you. When the widow Mrs Anne King was murdered in 1761 by her lodger Theodore Gardelle, the *Gentleman's Magazine* report concluded:

> On reflection, upon reading this dreadful narrative, will probably rise in the mind of the attentive reader; the advantages of virtue with respect to our social connections, and the interest that others take in what befalls us. It does not appear that, during all the time Mrs *King* was missing, she was enquired after by one relation or friend... But who is there of honest reputation, however poor, that could be missing a day, without becoming the subject of many interested enquiries, without exciting solitude and fears, that would have had no rest till the truth had been discovered, and the injury, if any, had been avenged.

WORK

B Y THE MID-EIGHTEENTH CENTURY, trade was beginning to lose its taint, as John Fransham noted in his 1740 essay, *The World in Miniature*:

Gentlemen are those properly, who, being descended of a good Family, bear a Coat of Arms, without any particular Title. Formerly Trading degraded a Gentleman, and now a thriving Tradesman becomes a Gentleman by the happy Return of his Trade. As to Merchants, the Founders of Trade, and of the Nation's Wealth, they deserve indeed to be ranked among Gentlemen; therefore many Gentlemen born, take upon them this Profession, without any Prejudice or Blemish to their Birth: Nay, 'tis common with us, for Gentlemen's and Merchants Sons and Daughters to inter marry. In short, the Title of Gentlemen is given in *England* to all that distinguish themselves from the common Sort of People, by a good Garb, genteel Air, good Education, Wealth, or Learning.

It was precisely this type of mutually self-serving inter-marriage (suggesting a lack of respect let alone love from either spouse) that Hogarth lampooned in his *Marriage A-la-Mode*. A wealthy merchant's daughter and the son from an old but impoverished aristocratic family are sacrificed for the social pretensions of the former, and the greed – or rather shameless freeloading – of the latter. However, in reality such wealth and status was vital to the realm of work, in that the wealthy and leisured were always in need of lawyers and physicians and had expendable income for luxury goods.

Opposite: Samuel Scott, *A Thames Wharf, c.* 1750s. Lying to the east of the Tower, the Pool of London was the hub of coastal and overseas trade.

Below: William Hogarth, 'Scene I: The Marriage Settlement' from *Marriage A-la-Mode*, 1743. The gouty Earl of Squander (right) points to his 'illustrious' family tree. Outside, construction on his Palladian house continues with the Alderman's cash.

J. M. W. Turner, *Harewood House from the North East*, 1797. Harewood House was built between 1759 and 1771 for Edwin Lascelles, 1st Baron Harewood (1713–95), and designed by architects John Carr and Robert Adam.

The Beckfords (see pages 25 and 26) were an example of trade transforming a family's status. Another example was the Lascelles family of London and Yorkshire. Henry Lascelles, the English-born Barbados plantation owner, slave trader and director of the British East India Company had gross assets of £392,704 by the time of his death (possible suicide) in 1753. This was divided between his second son, Daniel, who took over the business Lascelles and Maxwell, and his first son, Edwin, who was lord of the manor of the two family estates of Gawthrope and Harewood. It was Edwin, 1st Baron Harewood, who oversaw the building of the magnificent Harewood House.

William Hogarth, *The Bench*, 1753–4.

Many men from the traditional middling professions, such as the law, medicine, the church, publishing or to an extent general builders might continue to work for most of their lives – particularly whilst there was a wife, young family or unmarried children to keep – but aspired and acquired the status of gentleman. To this group can also be added artists, writers and architects, who might live by the dexterity of their pen and pencil but stressed the learning required of their profession, a knowledge of classical design, history and literature for example, which elevated their craft to an intellectual and genteel pursuit.

William Hogarth, 'Plate 1: The Fellow 'Prentices at their Looms' from *Industry and Idleness*, 1747.

Sir John Vanburgh and Sir James Thornhill (writer/architect and artist respectively) at the beginning of the century and Sir Joshua Reynolds (artist) towards the end were the exemplars. In the first half of the eighteenth century, in addition to the Guilds and trade/professional associations, the professional man could do worse than join the Freemasons (Grand Lodge formed in 1717). Most Grand Masters came from the aristocracy, and it could include royalty (Frederick Prince of Wales and his brother the Duke of Cumberland) and politicians (Sir Robert Walpole) amongst its members. This society allowed for different social strata and professions to mix freely without the formality of introduction and the usual restrictions that existed outside the lodge providing dignity, mutual support and networking.

William Hogarth, *Anne Hogarth*, c. 1740.

Some men from relatively lowly origins could amass sizeable fortunes via the luxury trades, for example dress silk. *Common Sense or The Englishman's Journal* (24 February 1739) announced, 'At his House in Pater-noster Row, Spitalfields, Mr. Robert Harris, an eminent Weaver, said to have died worth 40,000 l' and similarly in the *General Advertiser* (10 September 1745) died 'at his House in Brick-lane Spitalfields, Mr. Venner, an eminent Silk-Throwster, of a very considerable Fortune'.

No. 27 Fournier Street (formerly No. 21 Church Street), Spitalfields, built by the eminent weaver Peter Bourdon c. 1725. The silk looms were later located in purpose-built studios on the garret (third floor) level.

The bookseller, Thomas Guy, amassed a fortune so enormous that he could pay for and then endow a hospital (see pages 67–9). Medicine and associated professions could be extremely lucrative. Daniel Graham, apothecary to George II and George III, resided at 11 Pall Mall. His wealth is more than evident from the elegant attire of his four children in Hogarth's group portrait of 1742 (see page 20). The physician Dr Richard Mead built up a practice that 'during almost half a century, produced near 8000 guineas per annum; but not withstanding this prodigious gain, he did not die rich.' This, according to the *Gentleman's Magazine*, was mainly due to his expenditure on art.

As has been stated before, even success was precarious, particularly, as noted by contemporary observers, if the party concerned was living beyond his means in an attempt to ape his betters. This certainly appears to have been the case for the merchant John Perrott who owned by all accounts a thriving linen draper's shop on Ludgate Hill. On 21 October 1761 'he was indicted, for that he having become a bankrupt; after which he did conceal, embezzle, and remove his effects, to above the value of 20 l.' In law, if a man declared himself bankrupt and within a certain time period correctly itemised all his property (for the purposes of his creditors) then his slate was effectively wiped clean. However, the *Proceedings of the Old Bailey* outlined the extent of Perrott's deception and debt which, in less than twelve months, was estimated as £26,000–£27,000. What was he spending his credit on? The ordinary (or priest) at Newgate Prison observed Perrott 'was visited from the first, by a gay dressy lady, whom in my simplicity and ignorance, I took for his wife.' He continues, 'This specious figure of alluring aspect and well coloured cheek, usually came several times a week, in a coach, or post-chaise, attended by a servant in livery, or a maid servant, or both, in order to keep up his spirits.' Perrott admitted to, 'Expences attending the connection I had with the fair sex,' of £5,500. He was found guilty and hanged at Tyburn on 12 November 1761.

Although it was not unknown for women to work in 'honest' professions – particularly single or widowed women – they were excluded from the majority of male trades and professions. In *A City Full of People* (1994), Peter Earle states that independent women ran businesses associated with food and drink (such as distilleries or taverns and inns), or retail, selling haberdashery, clothing, textiles and luxury items. Pawnbroking was also popular. Women engaging in traditional male professions were less common, but some female merchants, sword-cutlers, perfumers, booksellers and even gunpowder suppliers are listed. William Hogarth's single sisters, Anne and Mary, jointly owned a children's clothing shop until Mary's death in 1741. Their trade card announced that they sold, 'ye best & most Fashionable Ready Made Frocks, sutes of Fustian, Ticken & Holland, stript Dimmity & Flanel, Wastcoats, blue & canvas Frocks & bluecoat Boys Dra[we]rs Likewise Fustians, Tickens, Hollands, white stript Dimitys, white & stript Flanels in ye piece; by Wholesale or Retale at Reasonable Rates.' Dorothy Mercier sold prints, stationery and artist materials from her shop at the Golden Ball in Windmill Street from 1745–70. Anna Maria Garthwaite was a successful freelance silk designer who lived and worked in Spitalfields from about 1730 until her death in 1763. Although she produced as many as eighty designs a year (see page 48) to commissions from master weavers and mercers, her wealth at death was approx £600, suggesting that designing silk was nowhere near as lucrative as producing and selling it.

Top: No. 2 Princelet Street, Anna Maria Garthwaite's house, Spitalfields.

Right: Allan Ramsay, *Dr Richard Mead*, 1747. Mead was also a supporter and governor of the new Foundling Hospital, see pages 69–70.

FOOD AND DRINK

B Y THE MID-GEORGIAN PERIOD, food (raw or cooked) and drink (which aside from water or milk were predominantly alcoholic or tea, coffee, chocolate) could be acquired both retail and wholesale from a variety of locations and businesses. The specialist markets included Smithfields (meat), Billingsgate (fish) in the City, and Covent Garden (fruit and vegetables) in the West End. Described in 1742 by the *Survey of London*, Leadenhall Market had three courts or yards: one predominantly for beef, which was given over to leather on Tuesday and wool on Thursday, a second selling veal, mutton and lamb and a third built in 1730 called 'New Market' or '*Nashe's* Rents' again used by butchers. Around these main yards were tenements for fishmongers, victuallers, poulterers, cheesemongers and cooks, the latter possibly to feed the market stallholders and workers. Another general market, Newgate Market (formerly 'St. Nicholas's shambles') close by St Paul's Cathedral, was described in 1770 as a:

> ...handsome market, commodious square piece of ground measuring 194 feet from east to west and 148 feet from north to south. In the middle is a market-house, under which are vaults or cellars, and the upper part of the building is employed as a kind of warehouse for the fruiterers, and the keepers of green-stalls by night. In the shops under this building tripe and other things are sold, and in the middle, near the market-house, are sold fruit and greens.

The most famous market and one that epitomises the transformation and diversity of Georgian London, was Covent Garden. The Great Piazza designed by Inigo Jones was in the seventeenth century an elegant aristocratic square. By the 1740s however, 'to its Disgrace is kept an Herb and Fruit Market; two Charity-schools, one Meeting [house]; a Parish Workhouse, two Bagnios, a Cold Bath, and a Playhouse'. The author of the *Survey of London* (1742 edition) notes

Opposite: Samuel Scott, *Covent Garden on a Market Day*, c. 1749–58. St Paul's Church can be seen at the far side of the Great Piazza.

A. C. Pugin and
T. Rowlandson,
'Billingsgate
Market' from
*The Microcosm
of London*, 1808.

with mounting disapproval that the dominance of the market within the square, 'has prov'd so very prejudicial to the magnificent Buildings thereof, that, instead of their being inhabited by Persons of the greatest Distinction as formerly, they are now in the Possession of Vintners, Coffeemen, and other such Inhabitants.'

Comestibles and luxury foodstuffs were purchased from specialist shops. In 1706 Thomas Twining took over Tom's Coffee House on the Strand near Temple Bar and began selling tea and coffee, wet and dry. By 1717 he had expanded his premises and created one of the earliest,

No. 3 St James's
Street, Berry
Bros & Rudd.

if not the first, dry tea and coffee shops (now 216 Strand; for his son see pages 17–8). Berry Bros & Rudd on St James's Street famed purveyors of wines and spirits, was originally and throughout the eighteenth century a grocers (established 1698 by the Widow Bourne); and just along Piccadilly, William Fortnum and Hugh Mason developed their business selling recycled candles from nearby St James's Palace (established 1707) to a quality grocers supplying the Royal Family from 1761.

The buying of food and drink for consumption at home was in the main the role of the housekeeper and/or cook in more affluent households, or the wife and mother. The number of publications for housekeepers and housewives during the eighteenth century is extensive – each running into several editions and revisions – which reveals the market for such books is no modern phenomenon. To highlight a few, Hannah Glasse's *The Art of Cookery, made Plain and Easy* (ten editions between 1747 and 1767), Sarah Jackson's *The director: or, young woman's best companion* (three editions between 1754 and 1770) and the Manchester confectioner Elizabeth Raffald's *The experienced English house-keeper, for the use and ease of Ladies, House-keepers, Cooks, &c* of 1769. They offered advice on every aspect of cooking and formal entertaining at home.

The Coffee Mill shop sign, No. 3 St James's Street, Berry Bros & Rudd. The original owner, Widow Bourne, traded under this sign.

Pickering Place, St James's Street. This beautiful little court is located behind Berry Bros & Rudd and is named after William Pickering (painter, stainer and grocer), son-in-law to the Widow Bourne. The courtyard and surrounding buildings were rebuilt by Pickering in the early 1730s.

Hannah Glasse's
*The Art of Cookery,
made Plain and
Easy,* London,
1747.

Some also included herbal medicines. Raffald's, dedicated to the Hon. Lady Elizabeth Warburton 'Whom the author lately served as House-keeper', although based on the table of a great house, could be used for inspiration or indeed aspiration by the middling sort. She explained staples for any household, the basic cooking methods for all meats, seafood and vegetables – boiling, broiling, braising, baking, roasting, stewing and frying – with pies, puddings, cakes and preserving, 'Pickling, Potting, Collaring, Wines, Vinegars, Catchups, Distilling'.

Revealing the array of food available, in Chapter XXI, 'How to market, and the Seasons of the Year…' Hannah Glasse described how to check for freshness in market meat ('To chuse Lamb…mind the Neck Vein; if it be an azure Blue it is new and good, but if greenish or yellowish, it is near tainting, if not tainted already'), as well as in-season meats, fruit and vegetables. In regard to what constituted a meal, Sarah Jackson listed the various courses or 'bill of fare' that could be served in each month of the year – taking April:

First Course. *Poultry*; as, Bisque of Pigeons, Rabbets or Chickens fricasy'd. *Fish*; as, Mackarel, with Gooseberry Sauce, if to be had; Carp, Tench &c. stew'd or boil'd. Beef boil'd, roasted, or stew'd.

Calf's-head or Knuckle of Veal, or Fowls with Bacon and Greens, as
Brocoli, Spinach, &c. Neck of Veal boil'd, with Rice. Ham and
Chickens, or Pigeons, with Brocoli, or other Greens. Chine of Veal,
or Leg of Lamb, with Spinach, boil'd or stew'd. *Scots* Collops. *Pastry*;
as Lumber-pye, Veal or Lamb-pye, &c.

Moving on to the second course:

Poultry; as, Green Geese. Ducklings roasted, or sucking Rabbets
Chickens and Asparagus. *Fish*; as Butter'd Sea-Crabs, fry'd Smelts,
roasted Lobsters and Prawns, Crab-fish, Marinated-fish, pickled
Salmon or Herrings, souc'd Mullets. Roast Lamb, with Cucumbers,
or *French* Beans, if to be had. *Pastry*; as Hot butter'd Apple-pye, Tarts,
Cheese-cakes, Custards, Rock of Snow and Syllabubs. *Fruit* of all
Sorts; as, Nonpareils, Pearmains, Russet Pippings, Bonchretian Pears,
&c. Cherries and Rasberries, if to be had.

For those who did not care for eating in – or for the sheer convenience
or joy of it – London provided a multitude of taverns, coffee houses
and dining houses ('chop' and 'beef-steak') located on every street
and in every part of the city. Coffee houses and taverns were the hub
of male social interaction: the acquiring of up-to-date information via
the daily newspapers, idle chat or topical debate with companions or
simply whoever was to hand, as well as eating and drinking. As a
gentleman in lodgings, Boswell had the facility to dine with his host,
but clearly preferred to do the rounds of the eateries about town. His
diary lists numerous such venues, including 'Dolly's Beefsteak-house'
near the Guildhall and Child's Coffee-house [near Ludgate Street],
where he 'breakfasted, read the political papers, and had some chat
with citizens.' Boswell described the allure as follows:

Ye Old Cheshire
Cheese, Fleet
Street, City of
London. The
tavern was rebuilt
in 1667 after the
Great Fire and
frequented by
Dr Johnson who
lived just north in
Gough Square.

A beefsteak-house is a most excellent
place to dine at. You come in there to a
warm, comfortable, large room, where
a number of people are sitting at table.
You take whatever place you find empty;
call for what you like, which you get
well and cleverly dressed. You may
either chat or not as you like. No-body
minds you, and you pay very reasonably.
My dinner (beef, bread and beer and
waiter) was only a shilling. The waiters

The Seven Stars, Carey Street (formerly Vere Street), near Lincoln's Inn Fields. Founded in 1602, it is a survivor of the Great Fire. In 1750 it was advertised that 'The True Cordial Quintessence of the Vipers', a cure for impotency and barrenness, could be purchased here.

make a great deal of money by these pennies. Indeed, I admire the English for attending to small sums, as many smalls make a great, according to the proverb.

Attributed to William Hogarth, *A Midnight Modern Conversation*, c. 1732. The drunken disarray of the gentlemen is emphasised by the orderly row of their hats hanging from nails in the panelling.

The core alcoholic beverages were beer and wine. Gin or 'Mother Geneva' was at this time a poor man's drink, distilled by anyone who had a fancy to, and from whatever they had to hand. It was potent stuff that addled the brain and was presumed to be a cause of escalating crime – thus the subject of much agonising by socially minded middling sorts. Hogarth's terrifying vision *Gin Lane* (1751) (page 4) helped to bring about the regulating 'Gin Act' of the same year. In contrast its companion, *Beer Street* celebrates the healthy and patriotic

William Hogarth,
Beer Street, 1751.
The rude health
of the comely
female street
sellers here
contrasts
dramatically with
the befuddled hag
in *Gin Lane*,
page 4.

alternative. Brewed in London and its environs including many
hospitals (for example St Bartholomew's and the Royal Chelsea), it
was not as alcoholic as the modern counterpart and considered
healthier than the water. Although the image of the standard Georgian
male has come to be a carousing drunkard, many commentators at
the time bewailed the abuse of alcohol by their fellows. One teetotal
writer in the *Gentleman's Magazine* (September 1754), witnessing a
rowdy night at a drinking club stated that he was unable to explain 'this
deliberate and assiduous sacrifice of time, health, and reason, which
is daily offered up by two millions of his fellow subjects.' He recalled
being asked, '"Mr. FitzAdam, you, who drink nothing but water, and
live much at home, how do you keep your spirits?" "Why, doctor," said
I, "as I never lowered my spirits by strong liquor, I don't want it to
raise them."'

FASHION

DESPITE THE FACT that Britain was technically at war with France for most of the period, Paris remained the innovative centre of fashion – with the finest silks and damasks and the most skilful tailors – to which the British aristocracy and to a lesser extent the middling sort looked for sartorial guidance. The following of French fashion was often slavish, sometimes grudging, for there was something decidedly unpatriotic about it, as the author Tobias Smollett observed in *Travels through France and Italy* (1766):

> The French, however, with all their absurdities, preserve a certain ascendancy over us, which is very disgraceful to our nation; and this appears in nothing more than in the article of dress. We are contented to be thought their apes in fashion; but, in fact, we are slaves to their taylors, mantua [dress]-makers, barbers, and other tradesmen.

As Smollet's comment suggests, amongst patrons of luxury goods and the arts in general, there was a bias in favour of all things foreign, from clothing to music, perpetuated by British travellers abroad, and those young males sent on the 'Grand Tour' in particular. Deemed a crucial element of a gentleman's training – the aspirant as well as the traditionally wealthy – this journey of years' rather than months' duration took in the modern-day glories of Venice and Paris (prostitution and fashion respectively) *en route* to the ancient and renaissance glories of Florence and Rome. They returned in their droves dazzled and enlightened, weighed down with Old Masters and antiquities, and kitted out from head to foot in the latest attire *á la parisien*. To quote Smollett once more:

When an Englishman comes to Paris, he cannot appear until he has undergone a total metamorphosis. At his first arrival he finds it necessary to send for the taylor, peruquier, hatter, shoemaker,

Opposite: Henry Pickering, *Portrait of Eleanor Frances Dixie, c. 1753.* The sitter wears a sack robe probably of Spitalfield's silk and for modesty, a fine lace 'fichu' to veil her décolletage.

Joseph Highmore, *The Family of Eldred Lancelot-Lee*, 1736. A middling landowning family near Bridgnorth, Shropshire, the Lees are presented in elegantly restrained fashion of the mid-1730s. Note the full-skirted coat of the eldest son (right) and the white loose robe of the mother (seated left).

Thomas Gainsborough, *Captain William Wade*, 1769. Wade, the illegitimate son of Field Marshall George Wade, was a master of ceremonies for the Assembly Rooms in Bath. He wears a flamboyant formal costume of red and gold silk. Note the hair 'buckles' and slimmed cut of his coat.

and every other tradesman concerned in the equipment of the human body. He must even change his buckles, and the form of his ruffles; and, though at the risque of his life, suit his cloaths to the mode of the season.

For most people, unwilling or unable to countenance the expense of the Grand Tour, the effects of it would still permeate all levels of fashionable and genteel society. And yet, although the lead came undeniably from Paris, there are still subtle and some significant differences in the costume worn in Britain from 1740–70. In the main, the style is less overtly extravagant and there was a greater emphasis on informality at home or out of doors. There was therefore for men, and to a lesser extent women, a distinction made between clothes worn for different types of activity – for example a fitted cut which restricted movement was more suited to a ball, and would not do for country sports. The unstiffened frock coat, originally a working man's coat, was adopted by fashionable men from the 1720s for sport or informal occasions. It was usually made from an unadorned cloth and unlike the formal coat, had a small collar.

By 1730, the full-bottomed powdered wig had shortened to a powdered long bob, with loose curls framing the face to the shoulder. Men still wore their own hair close-cropped or shaved (at home or at leisure they would wear a soft turban or velvet cap) but increasingly it was permissible to wear hair long and 'dressed' with or without powder, even on formal occasions, in place of a wig. A decade on, the fashionable wigs were now a 'bag' (formal) or 'tye' (hair drawn back and tied with a ribbon) with side roll curls or buckles (from the French *bouclé*), or your own hair in a similar style. The basic clothing for men had been established by the late seventeenth century; that is, three key pieces of coat, waistcoat and breeches. From the 1720s the coat lost its full skirt and large cuffs, gradually reducing down to a slimmer, fitted cut that curved back from the chest. Fabric weights and decoration also lightened from brocades and damasks to silk and fine woollen cloth. The waistcoat in turn shortened and slimmed, and could be a

No. 6 St James's Street, Lock & Co. In 1759, James Lock inherited his former master and father-in-law's hat business. In 1765 the business moved from the west side of St James's Street to No. 6.

Anna Maria Garthwaite, *Floral design of carnations and roses for a silk material to be woven at Spitalfields*, 1744.

simple wool or more ornate silk depending on the occasion. Breeches were usually, but not always, the same fabric as the coat, buttoned and buckled at the knee with a buttoned flap at the front. Stockings of wool, linen thread or silk and shoes, usually black leather with buckles (silver or even diamonds for best) completed the outfit. Underneath was worn a shirt and at the neck, a length of cloth called the stock.

Women's hair from 1740 was dressed up, either pulled back off the face and gathered up in curls at the back of the head, or by the late 1740s with curls falling almost to the shoulder at the back of the neck. Women habitually wore a white linen cap, sometimes decorated with lace or ribbon, which could be covered by a wide-brimmed hat (straw in the summer). By the late 1750s women were wearing hair ornaments of ribbon and feather pompoms. Into the 1760s, hair was still worn back from the face but gradually fuller and higher – sometimes plaited around the head or loosely plaited into a topknot or in a looped chignon. By the late 1760s women were using pads with their hair combed over to achieve the increasingly fashionable height, a style that reached its apogee in the 1770s and 1780s.

The dress, called a robe or gown, was described as 'open' or 'closed'; the former open at the front and requiring lacing, a

Johann Zoffany, *Andrew Drummond and his family*, c. 1769. Drummond (seated) was a London-based goldsmith and banker. The generational differences are evident in the style of male wigs and coats. Note also the 'higher' dressing of the female hair.

stomacher and underskirt or petticoat. The robe was either fitted at the back or had fabric falling from the shoulders, the latter known as a sack or *sacque* and the popular style in England from the 1730s to 1750s. White satin was particularly favoured as were the silk designs of Spitalfields such as the dainty patterns of clustered flowers from the 1740s (see opposite). Informal wear included simpler wrapping gowns, closed robes, or skirt and jacket ensembles. 'Morning Gowns' and 'Banjans' were informal items for both sexes (negligée dresses and dressing gowns).

Whether formal or informal, the gowns and robes were worn over hoops with various types of underskirt. Beneath this was worn a shift (loose shirt), stays (like a corset, ribbed with whalebone and laced) and hose or stockings of wool, linen or silk, gartered at the knee. Underwear in the modern sense was not worn (see page 21). Shoes were leather for everyday, or silk for formal occasions. Pearls and semi-precious stones were very popular for jewellery and hair ornaments. Cosmetics in the main were frowned upon amongst the middling sort – they were usually the preserve of prostitutes or dissolute aristocrats. Products for the skin could be purchased at an apothecary or made at home. Eliza Smith's *The Compleat Housewife* (from 1739) included recipes for lip salve which contained 'alkermes-root', butter, beeswax and claret: the latter must have acted as a 'rouge'. France was the centre of European perfume production and in England colognes or scented water were popular. If greater intervention was required, an advertisement in the *Morning Chronicle and London Advertiser* (27 May 1772) recommended:

T Hall, 'A Cosmetick water used by the Queen' from *The Queen's Royal Cookery*, fourth edition, London, 1729.

The TOILET of FLORA: or, a Collection of the most simple and approved methods of preparing baths essences, pomatums, powders, perfumes, sweet-scented waters, and opiates for the preserving and whitening of teeth, &c. With receipts for cosmetics of every kind, that can smooth and brighten the skin, give force to beauty, and take off the appearance of old age and decay. For the use of the Ladies.

TRANSPORT

THERE WERE two ways to travel in Georgian London: by land or by river. Either way, the citizen was at his or her most vulnerable when travelling, for London's streets were thronging with danger – everything from unruly animals being taken to market, to muggers and highwaymen. Because of its size and density, as well as the relative proximity of most areas of the city where the middling sort lived and/or worked, the cheapest and most popular mode of transport was to walk. Walking was also considered healthy. To avoid the dirt and bustle of a London street or inclement weather, a man or woman could take a sedan chair: a box-shaped object with hinged roof, windows and a door which was supported on two horizontal poles and carried by two 'chairmen' – compact enough to take passengers from their front hall to that of their destination (see opposite).

Above this were the hackney coaches (from the French *haquenee*, an ambling horse), which could be called up in the street or at a stand and hired on a distance (i.e. within London), and then time-related rate. The Hackneys were regulated by acts of parliament, which permitted only eight-hundred Hackney-Coaches and Hackney-Chairs to operate in London and Westminster: all of them licensed and displaying tin plates with their number. The drivers of unlicensed coaches were fined £5. According to *The pocket remembrancer; or, a concise history of the city of London, c.* 1750, the fare in London, 'or within 10 Miles thereof, is 10 sh.[illings] per Day, including 12 Hours to the Day; and by the Hour, 1 s. 6 d. for the first Hour, and 1 s. for every hour, afterwards.' *The book of coach-rates; or, hackney-coach directory* (1770) listed coach, chair and waterman rates, and the length of the principal streets in London allowing the traveller to calculate the fare, although the publication includes standard journeys, distance and fare. For example, Blackheath to St James's Palace Gate was just over 6 miles and 6 furlongs and therefore 5 shillings. Some stabled a horse (they could also be hired) and the very wealthy kept horses and a carriage.

Opposite:
John Collet, *Scene in a London Street,* 1770. Note the lady emerging from the sedan chair (right) and behind the Bath coach or 'Bath Fly'. The sign above, 'The New Bagnio' may indicate a 'Turkish bath' or bawdy house.

Joseph Nickolls, *View of Charing Cross and Northumberland House*, 1746. The central equestrian statue of King Charles I remains in situ at the north end of Whitehall (now Trafalgar Square). The entrance to the Strand is located behind it.

The key river transport for pedestrians were the small boats (river 'hackneys') operated by the watermen. Their trade thrived for one key reason: in 1740 London Bridge was the only bridge across the Thames in London (either the City or Westminster). In essentials, this bridge was the same structure that Shakespeare would have known: a continuous shamble of uneven buildings on a 'road' held up by nineteen supports or 'starlings'. The latter had been reinforced over the years so that by the mid-eighteenth century, the river water forced its way

Below: Samuel Scott, *Old London Bridge*, 1753. This view is of the east side from St Olave's stairs (seen to the left).

through narrow gaps. In 1739 however, after decades of petitioning, the foundations of a new bridge at Westminster were laid. Designed by the Swiss architect Charles Labelye, it connected the Palace of Westminster, the site of the Houses of Parliament, on the north bank to Lambeth Palace, the residence of the Archbishop of Canterbury on the south. Prior to this, anyone wanting to travel across from one bank to the other had to use the Westminster horse ferry, hire a waterman or brave the round trip up to London Bridge, over it and then down the other side. Unsurprisingly the Corporation of London and the watermen had been the chief opposition to the new bridge. No wonder, then, that the building of the bridge captured the imagination as one of the sights of the day, and its gradual development, arch by arch, across the river was recorded by the finest landscape painters in London at the time, Canaletto included. It opened at midnight on 17/18 November 1750, the *Whitehall Evening Post* declaring, ''Tis now allowed, by Judges of Architecture, to be one of the grandest Bridges in the World. On Sunday Westminster was all Day like a Fair, with People going to view the Bridge, and pass over it.'

In response to Westminster's elegant new bridge, the Corporation remodelled London Bridge, removing the buildings and opening up the central element. Despite the improvements, this bridge remained an obstruction to the free flowing of the river, particularly in winter. In 1762 Boswell observed, 'with a pleasing horror the rude and terrible appearance of the river, partly froze up, partly covered with enormous shoals of floating ice which often crashed against each other.' Blackfriars was the last bridge of the period to be built, opening at first for pedestrians in 1766 and then horses and vehicles by 1769.

Antonio Canaletto, *View of the Thames and Westminster Bridge, c. 1746–7*. The Abbey and Palace of Westminster located to the west (left) of the bridge with Lambeth Palace to the south-east (right). The river bustles with craft including river 'hackneys'.

Travelling by stagecoach was hazardous, partly because of the woeful state of the roads, unless 'turnpiked' or tolled, and partly the potential for robbery. Yet they were a fast, regular and convenient means of transport from distant parts of the capital as well as cities and towns around the country. The *Universal pocket-book* of 1740 lists destinations alphabetically, the tavern where the stagecoach and carriers left from, and which days. The Bath coach (or 'Bath Fly'; see page 50) for example, left from three different taverns, 'three cups bread street, M[onday] Th[ursday] wint[er]. M T[uesday] F[riday] sum[mer]. Bell savage ludgate hill M Th wint. M W[ednesday] F sum. One bell in the strand, M. Th wint. M W F sum.' Highwaymen are almost synonymous with our idea of the eighteenth century, none more so than Dick Turpin. Before he was hanged in York for horse theft in 1739, Turpin had lived a short but active career in the notorious Essex-based 'Gregory's Gang' as a housebreaker, mugger and murderer before upgrading to highway robbery:

> Last Monday Mr. Omar, of Southwark, riding from thence to Barnes, met, between Barnes-Common and Wandsworth, Turpin the Butcher, one of Gregory's Gang, with another Person, well mounted, and not caring for their Company, clapt Spurs to his Horse, in Hopes to have got from them, but the Rogues turn'd about, and coming up with him oblig'd him to dismount; and Turpin suspecting that he knew him, presented a Pistol, and would have shot him, but was prevented by the other, who pull'd his Pistol out of his Hande, after which they rode off. (*General Evening Post*, Thursday 17 July 1735)

The risks were great and if caught, hanging was inevitable. But the potential returns if the thief kept one step ahead of the law were enormous. Whether travelling on horseback or in a coach, travellers were vulnerable, particularly on lonely open land such as Hounslow Heath or Barnes Common, as Mr Omar discovered above, and often travelling with fine clothes, portable luxuries and cash. One of the most famous, rather than notorious, highwaymen of the period was James Maclaine or Maclean known as the 'Gentleman Highwayman' because of his essentially non-violent and polite manner. He was finally caught whilst trying to sell on stolen goods but had managed to elude capture by openly masquerading as a gentleman, as the *Gentleman's Magazine* reported in September 1750:

> Since the 27th of *July*, the conversation of the town has been so much turned upon the gentleman highwayman, that some account will be

expected of him. On that day Mr *James Maclean*, who had handsome lodgings in St *James's-street*, at two guineas a week, and passed for an *Irish* gentleman of 700 l. a year, was apprehended and carry'd before Justice *Lediard*.

The report continues with a list of one day's haul, from several robberies, and indicates the type of items that could be stolen, as well as the market for second-hand wigs and clothing, which made such crime so lucrative:

He was charged with robbing Mr *Higden* in the *Salisbury* Coach, near *Turnham Green*, on *June* 26, of his portmanteau and some money, and was detected by selling to Mr *Loader*, of *Monmouth-street*, in his said lodgings, Mr *Higden*'s coat, breeches, and waistcoat, the lace ripped off, which cloaths being advertised, occasioned the discovery, and there was found in his lodgings a perrywig, three pair of stockings, a pair of pumps, and a handkerchief, the property of Mr *Higden*, several other things taken from the said coach, and 20 purses, also the blunderbuss, and a remarkable coat of Ld *Eglington*'s who was robbed the same morning.

Crime should not pay. Maclean was hanged at Tyburn on 3 October 1750.

English School, *An Exact Representation of Maclaine the Highwayman Robbing Lord Eglington on Hounslow Heath on the 26th of June 1750.*

Overleaf: A mid-Georgian quayside. The docks in London, Bristol, Liverpool and other cities were busy with transatlantic trade, coastal traffic and fishing vessels. All needed provisioning, and ports became the focus for trades and industry supplying the vessels with victuals, goods and sailors.

RELAXATION AND ENTERTAINMENT

James Boswell wrote in 1762:

> The enemies of the people of England who would have them
> considered in the worst light represent them as selfish, beef-eaters,
> and cruel. In this view I resolved today to be a true-born Old
> Englishman. I went into the City to Dolly's Steakhouse in Paternoster
> Row and swallowed my dinner by myself to fulfil the charge of
> selfishness; I had a large fat beefsteak to fulfil the charge of beef-eating;
> and I went at five o'clock to the Royal Cockpit in St James's Park and
> saw cock-fighting for about five hours to fulfil the charge of cruelty.

It might seem incongruous to open a chapter on relaxation and
entertainment with blood sports but, as Boswell states, the English
were notorious for seeking and achieving both through violence. As
Eobald Toze observed in 1770, a 'kind of savageness frequently prevails
in their manners, manifesting itself in the bloody fights and diversions
usual among them.' Amongst some, cruelty to animals was a great
concern, because it was presumed that those who inflicted pain on
defenceless creatures would need little encouragement to move on
to their fellow humans. This was Hogarth's argument in his *Four Stages
of Cruelty* (1751): the child who tortures the dog becomes the youth
beating his horse, and as a man, murders his pregnant 'wife' and is
executed. To conclude, in 'Stage Four' the murderer's screaming
corpse is anatomised (see page 75). Cock-fighting was popular, like
horseracing, as a form of gambling. Boswell describes his evening at
the Royal Cockpit on Birdcage Walk as follows:

> ...a circular room in the middle of which the cocks fight. It is seated
> round with rows gradually rising. The pit and the seats are all covered
> with mat. The cocks, nicely cut and dressed and armed with silver heels,
> are set down and fight with amazing bitterness and resolution. Some of

Opposite:
Antonio
Canaletto, *The
Interior of the
Rotunda, Ranelagh*,
1754. Located at
Chelsea adjoining
the Royal
Hospital,
Ranelagh
gradually eclipsed
Vauxhall as *the
venue of fashion.*
The central
support of the
Rococo Rotunda
included
fireplaces for the
winter.

them were quickly dispatched. One pair fought three quarters of an hour. The uproar and noise of betting is prodigious. A great deal of money made a very quick circulation from hand to hand. There was a number of professed gamblers there. An old cunning dog whose face I had seen at Newmarket sat by me a while. I told him I knew nothing of the matter. 'Sir,' said he, 'you have as good a chance as anybody.'

Above: William Hogarth, *The Cockpit* (or *Pit Ticket*), 5 November 1759. The central figure is the blind Lord Albermarle Bertie who takes the bets, whilst the character to the right of him steals a token.

Boxing was seen as healthy, manly, and as English as roast beef. The two famous London boxers of the mid-century were George Taylor and Jack Broughton. The latter owned an amphitheatre and boxing academy for gentlemen on Oxford Road, near to Tottenham Court Road. The *Gentleman's Magazine*, indicating there was an interest in this sport amongst its readership, reported that on Thursday 9 April 1750:

Was fought at Broughton's amphitheatre, a very long battle between *Slack* the famous boxer of Norwich, and one *Field*, a sailor; it lasted an hour and 32 minutes at sheer boxing, without hugging, standing still, or above 4 falls in the whole. *Slack* by two cross buttock falls, seasonably given, got the victory.

The magazine later described a fight between Slack, the winner above, and Broughton himself. Expecting Broughton to win, a sizeable audience of the great and good had come to see and gamble on it:

The first 2 minutes the odds were 20 to 1 on Broughton's head, but Slack soon recovering himself beat his adversary blind, and following in blows obtain'd a compleat victory in 14 minutes, to the great mortification of the knowing ones, who were finely taken in, particularly a peer of the first rank, who betting 10 to 1 lost 1000 l. The money received at the door was 130 l. besides 200 tickets at a guinea each, and as the battle was for the whole house, 'tis thought that the victor cleared 600 l.

Of course, not everyone enjoyed cock-fighting, boxing nor indeed the other London 'entertainments' of viewing prisoners at Newgate, the insane at Bedlam Hospital or hangings at Tyburn. None of these were considered elevating – at best you might have called the experience life-affirming – but as Tyburn was the only non-charging amongst them, it can be presumed that many members of our middling sort did attend. Certainly, William Hogarth and his father-in-law, Sir James Thornhill, visited famous criminals in their cells to take a likeness, which was then replicated and sold as prints. And due to the celebrity of such people, the artist could gain some fame himself and earn a very tidy sum. Apparently 3,000 people visited James Maclean, the 'Gentleman Highwayman' in his Newgate cell. The practice was so well established that Boswell felt almost obliged to visit Newgate during his stay in London:

'Jack Broughton' (1705–89), from *Pierce Egan's Boxiana; or Sketches of ancient and modern pugilism; from the days of the renowned Broughton and Slack... London, 1812.*

I then thought I should see prisoners of one kind or other... I stepped into a sort of court before the cells. They are surely most dismal places. There are three rows of 'em, four in a row, all above each other. They have double iron windows, and within these, strong iron rails; and in these dark mansions are the unhappy criminals confined. I did not go in, but stood in the court, where were a number of strange blackguard beings with sad countenances, most of them being friends and acquaintances of those under sentence of death.

The practice of admitting the paying public in to Bethlem or Bedlam Hospital in Moorfields was famously depicted by Hogarth in *A Rake's Progress* (see page 11). It was condemned by the *Gentleman's Magazine* in 1748:

But those are fallen yet lower, who resort to an hospital, intended for the reception and for cure of unhappy lunatics, purely to mock at the nakedness of human nature, and make themselves merry with the extravagances that deface the image of the creator, and exhibit their fellow creatures, in circumstances of the most pitiable infirmity, debility and unhappiness.

By 1776 the practice had stopped, to the financial detriment of the hospital.

Hangings, which included the two-hour parade of the condemned from Newgate to Tyburn, were free and regular, and in the main the entertainment of the lower orders rather than middling. However, the author J. T. Smith wrote in 1828: 'I remember well, when I was in my

Antonio Canaletto, *The Grand Walk, Vauxhall Gardens*, c. 1751. The garden included supper boxes (left), a gothic orchestra (right), a Chinese pavilion, ruins and statues, as well as long avenues (similar to the Mall) where visitors promenaded.

eighth year, Mr. Nollekens [the sculptor] calling at my father's house in Great Portland-street, and taking me to Oxford-road to see notorious Jack Rann, commonly called "Sixteen-string Jack," go to Tyburn to be hanged [30 November 1774].' Perhaps the most unusual execution at Tyburn, and therefore one that would have attracted a large and diverse gathering of the curious, was that of Lord Ferrers on 5 May 1760 for murdering his steward. In *Remarkable trials and interesting memoirs, of the most noted criminals* (1765), it was observed that:

> the Procession proceeded to Tyburn, with great Solemnity. Through prodigious Crouds of Spectators, who all the Way crouded the Streets, and lined the Windows. As they were passing, his Lordship asked Mr. Vaillant [a sheriff] if he had ever seen so great a Concourse of People? And upon his answering in the Negative, he rejoined, 'I suppose it is because they never saw a Lord hanged before.'

If it was the first time, it was also the last.

Music was one of the great public and private forms of entertainment and Handel, one of the greatest composers and performers of the age, dominated the London music scene. On the decline of Italian opera by the early 1740s and the success of his *Messiah* (first performed in Dublin, 1742), he was encouraged to focus on English oratorio as his main theatre-based musical form, and the genre includes some of his most famous works. Not everyone liked the idea of religious texts performed in theatre: 'An *Oratorio* is an *Act of Religion*, or it is not; if it is, I ask if the *Playhouse* is a fit *Temple* to perform it in, or a Company of *Players* fit *Ministers* of *God's Word*' complained one member of the public in a letter sent to the *Universal Spectator*, 19 March 1743. In fact it was through the annual benefit performances in the chapel at the Foundling Hospital (see page 69–70) during the 1750s onwards that *Messiah* achieved its unrivalled position in the London and then national consciousness. Handel's fame was such that even a rehearsal of his music to celebrate the Treaty of Aix-la-Chapelle (terminating the War of the Austrian Succession in 1748) could attract huge attention: 'FRIDAY 21. Was performed at *Vauxhall Gardens* the rehearsal of the music for the fireworks, by a band of 100 musicians, to an audience of above 12000 persons (tickets 2s. 6d). So great a resort occasioned such a stoppage on *London-Bridge*, that no carriage could pass for 3 hours.'

'Vauxhall Gardens' mentioned above (revived in 1738) was one of a number of pleasure gardens, which also included Chelsea (Ranelagh, established 1742) and Marylebone (redeveloped for formal music in 1738–9). To maintain a level of respectability they charged an entrance fee of between 2 shillings and 2 shillings and 6 pence. The gardens included long walks, supper boxes and exotic buildings for concerts – the grandest of which was the Rococo Rotunda at Ranelagh where Mozart performed in 1765.

Since the Restoration of Charles II (1660) London theatre had thrived, although, like all walks of life, it was sensitive to foreign invasion.

J. Kip after T. Badeslade, *Tunbridge Wells*, early eighteenth century. A view of the 'Walks', with the shops (left) built in the 1680s (see also page 64).

William Hogarth, *David Garrick as Richard III*, 1745.

As a riposte to recently imported art forms (such as Italian opera) as well as a brazen contemporary political and social satire, *The Beggar's Opera* (see page 19) swaggered on to the stage at Lincoln's Inn Fields in 1728: it was English, it was very bawdy and it was a hit. As Handel discovered, things were never quite the same again. This desire to promote home-grown culture instigated something of a revival for the works of Shakespeare, spearheaded by Dr Johnson's friend and compatriot, David Garrick. As Handel dominated music, so Garrick came to dominate theatre. A barnstorming performance of Shakespeare's *Richard III* in 1741 launched his career – Hogarth produced an equally barnstorming portrait of him in the role. At ease in comic and tragic roles, he was immediately credited for introducing a new realism and sensitive interpretation to the stage. Through business acumen, charm and a well-orchestrated media campaign (including Hogarth's portrait), he did much to elevate and dignify the acting profession.

Unknown artist, *The remarkable Characters…at Tunbridge Wells*, 1748. The characters include Dr Johnson, Mr David Garrick, Mr Beau Nash and Mr William Pitt.

As a brief respite from the metropolis and its hurly-burly, a sojourn at a spa town was a popular and often annual activity for many Londoners. William Maitland noted in his *The History of London* (1739):

The modern Diversions us'd by the Inhabitants of this City and Suburbs, are, that the principal Part of them in Summer, devesting themselves of urbanick Cares, repair to their fine Country Seats, and Gardens, where the Beauties of Nature display themselves, amidst the glorious Harmony of a rural Choir. Whilst others resort to *Bath*, *Tunbridge*, *Scarborough*, and other Places of Gaiety and Pleasure; where some too often divert themselves with Gaming, at the Expence, and sometimes Ruin of their Families.

Both visitors and entertainments in spa towns like Bath (Somerset) and Tunbridge Wells (Kent) were dragooned by a master of

ceremonies, such as Richard 'Beau' Nash (1674–1762), Ralph Allen and Captain William Wade (d.1809, see page 46) who exerted huge influence – effectively deciding who was in and who was out. No detail was beyond their attention, even down to the selection of dancing partners at the Assemblies. Between 1735 and 1762 Tunbridge Wells, under the self-appointed leadership of Nash and less than 40 miles from the capital, became a very popular resort. An engraving entitled *The remarkable Characters...at Tunbridge Wells* (1748) depicts the Walks (now the Pantiles). Protocol dictated, as defined by Nash, that gentry occupied the 'Upper Walks' or colonnade, everyone else the 'Lower'. Bath, however, for fashionable society and health, was and continued to be the principal spa town throughout the century. Building work alone during this period attested to its unrivalled status. We may think of Bath as the city of Jane Austen, but many of its architectural icons were created in the mid-eighteenth century: the Baths and Pump Room (see also page 76), the principal Assembly Rooms (John Wood the Elder 1728, extended 1750), the Circus (John Wood the Elder, built 1754–68), the Royal Crescent (John Wood the Younger, built 1767–74) and Pulteney Bridge (Robert Adam, completed in 1773).

J. Fayram, 'The Pump Room adjoining the Kings Bath' from *Four Views of the Hot Baths*, 1738–9. This building can be seen to the left in the engraving on page 76.

John Robert Cozens, *The Circus, Bath*, 1773. As seen here, originally the Circus was paved. The Royal Crescent lies just to the west via Brock Street.

CHARITY AND CITIZENSHIP

I N THE *Covent Garden Journal* of June 1752, Henry Fielding wrote, 'Charity is in fact the very characteristic of this nation at this time. – I believe we may challenge the whole world to parallel the examples which we have of late given of this sensible, this noble, this Christian virtue.' Despite the pride and even optimism evident in this statement, Fielding was not complacent that all mid-Georgian ills had been alleviated through private charity. It should be emphasised that no one at this time considered it the responsibility of the Government to provide for the poor, the needy, the sick or the homeless. In the main charity derived from the individual, managed by a collective of like-minded citizens. By 1752, Fielding could indeed point to some extraordinary acts of charity in the shape of hospitals for a plethora of ailments and circumstances, charity schools for boys and girls and benevolent funds for a variety of trades and professions. The 'Fund for the Support of Decay'd Musicians' (1738) was founded and supported by Handel on discovering the destitute children of his former oboist. Although monarchy and aristocracy contributed to these endeavours, lending any cause no matter how challenging or 'distasteful' a glamour and legitimacy, it was the middling sort who were the main drivers in the establishment, providing the ongoing funding (by voluntary subscription) and administration of such charities – fuelled by either religious imperatives or humanitarianism (or both), as well as the personal pleasure of doing good and purging the soul of vanity and selfishness. As one anonymous writer observed in the *Gentleman's Magazine* (1740), 'Charity is more advantageous to him that giveth, than to him that receiveth.' In addition, and evident in Handel's practical response to the plight of destitute musicians and their families, there must have been an element of 'there but for the Grace of God go I.'

General hospitals founded in this manner during the early to mid-Georgian period included Guy's in Southwark (1721), the Middlesex Infirmary (1745), and the London Hospital in Whitechapel (1752).

Opposite:
Balthasar Nebot,
Captain Thomas Coram, 1741.

Edward Penny,
The Marquess of Granby relieving a sick soldier, 1764. The General was famed for his compassion and care of his men.

Nathaniel Hone, *John Wesley*, c. 1766. In 1743 Wesley drew up the 'General Rules' of his new movement: that members 'should continue to evidence their desire of salvation … by doing no harm, by avoiding evil of every kind … doing good of every possible sort, and, as far as possible to all'.

These were accompanied by specialist hospitals for venereal diseases (the Lock, 1746), the insane (St Luke's in Old Street, 1751), and 'lying-in' or childbirth (Long-acre, 1749, City of London, 1750 and the General (later Queen Charlotte, 1752). The greatest example of individual philanthropy, and one that continued to amaze commentators decades after its foundation, was that of Guy's Hospital. In the 'Historical Description of Guys Hospital' published in the *Gentleman's Magazine* in 1784 the author notes, 'This hospital in Southwark, for the cure of sick and lame persons, was founded by Mr. Thomas Guy. A citizen and bookseller of London, who from a small beginning amassed an immense fortune, by his industry and frugality,' and it should also be said, canny investment in stocks and shares. The author continues:

He was never married, and had no near relations; and therefore towards the close of his life, considering how he should dispose of his wealth, after many ruminations, resolved to be the founder of the most extensive charity ever established by one man… The expense of erecting and furnishing this hospital amounted to the sum of 18,793 l. 16s. great part of which he expended in his own life time; and the sum he left to endow it amounted to 219,499 l.

If we consider that about the same time the annual salary of the first Lord of the Treasury (one of the highest Government offices in the land) was £4,000, this is a vast fortune for a humble bookseller to have accrued (albeit without the expense of a family) and an extremely generous donation.

Another extraordinary charitable foundation during this period (more for the subject than anything else) was the Foundling or 'Hospital for the Maintenance and Education of Exposed and Deserted Young Children'. The disturbing regularity with which infants were abandoned or even murdered was due in great part to the opprobrium associated with illegitimacy and the high value of a good character and unsullied reputation in unmarried females. The shame, it was often said, could therefore overcome maternal, moral or even religious imperatives – being cast into Hell's fire a lesser fear than being cast out of 'decent society'. And it should not be presumed that the middling and even aristocratic women were immune. The mother of the most famous foundling after Moses, the eponymous hero of Henry Fielding's *Tom Jones* (1749), is discovered at the end of the novel to be the unmarried sister of Tom's guardian, Mr Allsworthy, and therefore a well-to-do, god-fearing woman rather than the 'hussy' and 'wicked slut' as presumed all along. Allsworthy's generosity and 'Christian virtue' in viewing Tom as a defenceless infant – rather than the symbol of depravity – and to adopt him as his own despite the inevitable raising of genteel eyebrows, was an exemplar for all of Fielding's readership.

The Foundling Hospital – which received its Royal Charter in 1739, and from 1745 occupied an open site just north of the city in Lamb's Conduit Fields – was in fact the first of its kind in England. It had been presumed that a refuge for unwanted children would simply encourage debauchery and sexual relations outside of marriage – in all levels of society – and therefore a scheme to deal with the terrible waste of human life remained unresolved. The unwanted children who

William Toms after Robert West, *Bird's Eye View of Guy's Hospital, c. 1756*. The statue of Thomas Guy can be seen in the courtyard, centre.

were abandoned rather than murdered fell prey to gangs of street criminals and prostitution, stirring one petitioner, Thomas Bray, to ask in 1728, 'how far might every Individual be rendered useful to the Publick, instead of being the Pests of the Community, as remaining in their present State they are likely to prove!' It took

Samuel Wale, *Perspective View of the Foundling Hospital...*, 1749. This image depicts women entering the hospital with their infants. Due to its popularity, the governors soon introduced a balloting system using coloured balls: white (admitted), red (pending), black (rejected).

another determined and self-made man, a shipwright called Thomas Coram, twenty years of petitioning to finally establish a refuge for unwanted children. His success was partly due to compassion for the welfare of the children, but in greater part to the stated aim of the charity to turn a social nuisance into honest, hardworking citizens.

In this way the Foundling was akin to the many charity schools that existed in London. A table published in the *Gentleman's Magazine* in 1785 stated that 160 such schools were founded between 1688 and 1767: fourteen during the reign of George II and four during the first seven years of the reign of George III. Although there was a genuine desire to provide for and educate the poor in middling-sort philanthropy, nonetheless, there was no romantic idea that the poor should rise above their rightful place in society. 'Debates in the Senate of LILLIPUT' i.e. Parliament, were published in the *Gentleman's Magazine*, and one topic in October 1740 was the many charity schools, within which:

Children of the Poor receive an Education disproportion'd to their Birth. This has often no other Consequences than to make them unfit for their Stations by placing them in their own Opinion above the Drudgery of daily Labour, a Notion which is too much indulg'd, as Idleness co-operating with Vanity, can hardly fail to gain Ascendant, and which sometimes prompts them to support themselves by Practices not only useless but pernicious to Society.

In a statement echoed in the petitions for the Foundling Hospital, the speaker suggests that a proportion from every school should be allotted to the Sea Service.

Charities were of course open to abuse, even by the traditionally honourable, upstanding middling sort. In the *Proceedings of the Old Bailey* of 3 June 1742 we find a Henry Rooke:

indicted for defrauding the Corporation for the Relief of Poor Clergyman's Widows of several Sums of Money, by means of false Certificates, having receiv'd five Pounds Annually for 22 Years last past, as a gift to his Mother, she being the Widow of a Clergyman Deceas'd, pretending her alive when in fact she has been Dead all the while, he pleaded not Guilty, but afterwards begg'd leave to retract his former Plea, and pleaded Guilty.

For his pains, he was exposed to public ridicule in the pillory, which involved being pelted by onlookers with whatever came to hand.

With so many good causes, and the social requirement for charitable sensibility, the middling sort could be forgiven for suffering from the occasional bout of donor fatigue. As the satirical author of 'Advice from a Father to a Son' in the *Gentleman's Magazine* (1760) suggests:

> …as the mad extravagance of the age is *charity,* and you must meet with frequent temptations, and earnest solicitations, to squander your money in that way, I shall, in the first place, give you some instructions in the *art of parrying a charitable subscription.* The want of this necessary art has been a great misfortune to many people I could name you. For besides parting with their money against their will, they got the character of being charitable, which drew upon them fresh applications from other quarters, multiplying by success, and creating endless vexation.

John Sanders, *The Foundling Hospital Chapel looking West,* 1773. The chapel was the venue for the annual *Messiah* benefit. When the hospital was demolished, the organ case and Coram's remains (buried beneath the altar) were moved to St Andrew's Church, Holborn.

His answer? First rule, 'to like the charity, but dislike the mode of it'. If that fails, the second rule, 'to like some other charity better' and lastly, 'to insinuate (but without saying it in plain terms) that you either will contribute, or have already contributed handsomely, tho' you do not subscribe.' Sound advice perhaps for victims of 'chugging' (charity mugging) the length of twenty-first-century Oxford Street.

Cujus octavum trepidavit ætas Claudere lustrum

HEALTH

THE BENEFITS to general health of regular exercise and moderation in rich food and alcoholic drink were well known in the Georgian period. Dr George Cheyne in his *An Essay of Health and Long Life* (1724) presented a clear programme for a healthy lifestyle, which would in turn increase the likelihood of a long and happy life. The quantities of food and drink consumed, for example, should be proportionate to requirement. In regard to exercise he considers walking 'the most *natural*, as it would be also the most *useful*' and horse riding 'the most *Manly*, the most *Healthy*, and the least *laborious*' whilst 'shaking the whole *Machine*, promoting an universal *Perspiration* and Secretion of all the *Fluids*'. Also recommended was the 'violent and sudden Shock' of cold-bathing stimulating '*Circulation, full, free* and *open*, thro' all the *Capillary Arteries*, is of great Benefit towards *Health* and *Long Life*.' Dr Cheyne's observations and recommendations did not find favour with all his fellow scientists at the Royal Society, but the popularity of his *Essay* is clear from the seven editions produced in its first year.

It should be noted that when ill, the middling sort did not go to the hospitals (which were for the poor) but were tended at home and visited there by a physician. For the sick, Hannah Glasse recommended in her *The Art of Cookery* beef or mutton broth, 'Scragg of Veal', boiled chicken or a beef drink: 'Take a Pound of lean Beaf, take off the Fat and Skin, cut it into Pieces, put it into a Gallon of Water, with the Under-crust of a Penny-loaf, and very little Salt, let it boil till it comes to two Quarts; then strain off, and it is a very hearty Drink.' Light, warm drinks were particularly recommended, such as 'Barley Water. Put a quarter of a Pound of Pearl-Barley into two Quarts of Water, let it boil, and skim it very clean, boil half away, and strain it off. Sweeten to your Palate, but not too sweet, and put in two Spoonfuls of White Wine; drink it luke-warm.'

Georgian newspapers were crammed with advertisements recommending elixirs and tinctures, guaranteed to cure a gamut of

Opposite
William Hogarth,
*Francis Matthew
Schutz in his Bed*,
1755–60. Nursing
a hangover,
Schutz vomits
into a bowl.
Legend has it this
unflattering
portrait was
commissioned by
Schutz's wife to
shame him into a
healthier lifestyle.

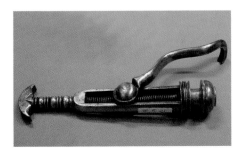

Dental Pelican, Heister's pattern, c. 1750. The 'claw' hooks over the decayed tooth, the fulcrum is placed against the gum, and then the 'endless screw' mechanism is tightened by turning the metal handle. It would have been an extremely painful process.

conditions and diseases. On 11 August 1752 an announcement in the *General Advertiser* wished 'to acquaint the public of some remarkable Cures done by Dr. Griffis's FAMOUS SUGAR CAKES for the WORM' concluding with some extraordinary testimonials. For example, Edmund Buttler, Carpenter 'by taking these Sugar Cakes, brought away a vast Quantity of Worms, like Toads, Lobsters, Shrimps and Caterpillars...' and a unfortunate boy who 'voided a vast Quantity of Worms, two in particular like a Hog, with black Eyes, and Legs, and a Tale like a serpent, and liv'd five Days after voided.' It is difficult to imagine anyone believing this.

Halitosis and tooth loss were a constant concern, predicated by a poor diet with an excess of sugar and primitive dental care. William Addis created the first mass-produced brush in 1780. Teeth were rubbed with various substances including soot and bicarbonate of soda. Tinctures for strong teeth, healthy gums and fresh breath were some of the most popular health related advertisements in Georgian newspapers:

> The most Delightful Fragrant TINCTURE for the Breath, Teeth and Gums. At once using makes the BREATH most charmingly fine,

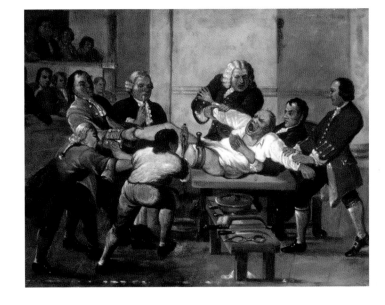

Unknown artist, An amputation, probably at St Thomas's Hospital, c. 1760. The tourniquet was introduced in 1674 allowing for control of blood flow. Before anaesthesia, alcohol was used to dull the pain and surgeons were rated by their speed.

sweet, and pleasant, the Teeth perfectly white, clean and beautiful, and is the most certain Cure for the Scurvy in the Gums in the World. (*Daily Gazeteer,* 8 February 1740)

Women could take a wonder pill that appeared to cure everything from period pain to symptoms of the menopause. Dr John Hooper's Female Pills under Royal Letters Patent,

cleanse, purify, and cause a free Circulation of the Blood, when in a manner stagnated; opens those Obstructions which Virgins are so liable to, and bring Nature into its proper Channel; whereby Health is recovered, and the Patient that look'd like Death restored to a lively Complexion... shou'd be taken by all Women at the Age of Forty-five or Fifty, to prevent those Disorders that usually attend them at that Time.

Mid-eighteenth-century amputation set.

Both Boswell and Johnson suffered from what we would now call depression, in Johnson's case profound melancholy. Boswell recalled Dr Johnson 'advised me to have constant occupation of mind, to take a great deal of exercise, and to live moderately; especially to shun

William Hogarth, 'The Reward of Cruelty' from *The Four Stages of Cruelty,* 1751. The highwayman James Maclean was not dissected at Surgeon's Hall but Hogarth includes his skeleton top right for topicality.

After Thomas Robins Senior, *View of the King's and Queen's Baths*, 1747. The structure in the centre of the King's Bath was called the 'Kitchen' because of the heat. There was seating and shelter for bathers. Those who were cured by the waters would hang their unwanted crutches on the 'Kitchen'.

drinking at night. "Melancholy people," said he, "are apt to fly to intemperance, which gives a momentary relief but sinks the soul much lower in misery."' Announcements professed cures for melancholy such as the 'Noble Elixir for Hypochondriack Melancholy in Men, and the Hysterick Disease or Vapours in Women' which 'Induces a new Train of chearful [sic] and pleasant Ideas, instead of those deep and black Thoughts, those direful Apprehensions that so tenaciously dwelt upon the Soul, clouded the Understanding, and destroy'd all Notion of ever receiving Comfort again'.

As Johnson himself had commented, excessive consumption of alcohol was seen as a contributing factor, if not the cause, of countless complaints including melancholy and gout, the medical condition perhaps most associated with the eighteenth century. Acute inflammatory arthritis caused by high levels of uric acid in the blood, gout was considered the 'rich man's disease' because of a demonstrable link to lifestyle and rich diet. Spa water was often promoted as both a means to alleviate the symptoms and as a cure, as the following example from an essay on the benefits of Bath's waters in the *Gentleman's Magazine* in August 1763 argues:

> George Long, at the age of 52, had suffered by the gout and stone more than 20 years; he was pained in every joint, his fingers became crooked, his right knee, hips, and back motionless by calculous matter which was deposited in every joint. He was bedridden, his thirst was intolerable, his appetite lost, his skin shrivelled, his face meagre, his hair grey, and his flesh so emaciated and flaccid, that he could throw the calf of his leg over his shinbone; with all this, he had a perpetual sharpness of urine; and his water, if left a day or two in the vessel, formed a strong crust on the sides of it, as thick as a half crown.

The author goes on to describe Mr Long's regime in Bath, both drinking and bathing in the water and, 'in some months his complaints all gradually vanished…his motions were all free and vigourous, and he obtained a fleshy hale habit of body, a vigourous eye, and a ruddy, plump, youthful face; he lived several years afterwards, and did not relapse.'

Surgery, once perceived as no better than butchery, developed during this period. At the beginning, William Cheselden published a popular student manual *The Anatomy of the Human Body* (first published 1713, 11th edition 1792) and later his *Osteographia* (1733). During the 1720s he developed a fast and highly successful technique for removing bladder stones. Anatomy schools flourished. In 1746 William Hunter, physician and 'midwife', advertised courses where 'Gentlemen may have the opportunity of learning the Art of Dissecting'. But anatomists needed bodies. The obvious source was executed criminals, but there was often an unseemly tussle between the surgeon's men and the criminal's family and/or the mob at Tyburn. To play on this fear of dissection as a deterrent, the Murder Act of 1752 decreed that all such corpses should be hung in chains, or given up to the surgeons and their black arts.

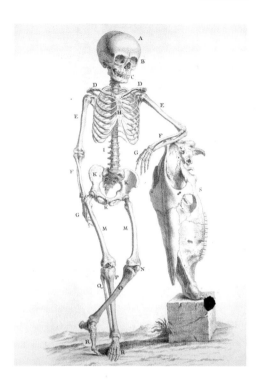

Top: Plate XXXIII 'A skeleton', from William Cheselden's *Osteographia, or the Anatomy of the bones*, London, 1733.

Bottom: Robert Edge Pine, *William Hunter*, c. 1760.

PLACES TO VISIT

Benjamin Franklin House, 36 Craven Street, London, WC2N 5NF.
www.benjaminfranklinhouse.org (pages 24, 25–7)

Building of Bath Collection, The Countess of Huntingdon's Chapel,
The Vineyards, Bath, BA1 5NA. www.bath-preservation-trust.org.uk

Christ Church (Spitalfields), Commercial Street, London, E1 6LY.
www.ccspitalfields.org

At the heart of Spitalfields, Christ Church was designed by Nicholas
Hawksmoor and built between 1714 and 1729.

Compton Verney, Warwickshire, CV35 9HZ. www.comptonverney.org.uk

Compton Verney is a stunning Grade I listed Robert Adam mansion located
in 120 acres of spectacular parkland. The wonderful collection includes
Canaletto's paintings of Vauxhall and Ranelagh Gardens (pages 58, 62).

Dennis Severs' House, 18 Folgate Street, Spitalfields, London, E1 6BX.
www.dennissevershouse.co.uk

This early eighteenth-century house has been transformed into an
extraordinary, theatrical experience, including sounds and smells.

Dr Johnson's House, 17 Gough Square, London, EC4A 3DE.
www.drjohnsonshouse.org (page 10)

Fairfax House, Castlegate, York, YO1 9RN. www.fairfaxhouse.co.uk

Designed by John Carr and built in 1762, Fairfax House is one of the finest
Georgian townhouses in Britain, with spectacular interiors and collections.

The Foundling Museum, 40 Brunswick Square, London, WC1N 1AZ.
www.foundlingmuseum.org.uk

In tandem with the history of the Foundling Hospital, the museum
contains an extraordinary collection of eighteenth-century fine art.
(pages 13, 68, 69–71)

Gainsborough's House, 46 Gainsborough Street, Sudbury, Suffolk, CO10 2EU.
www.gainsborough.org

The artist's birthplace. (pages 14, 46)

Geffrye Museum, 136 Kingsland Road, London, E2 8EA.
www.geffrye-museum.org.uk

A series of period rooms show the changing style of the English
domestic interior from 1600 to the present day.

Guy's Hospital, Great Maze Pond, London, SE1 9RT.
www.guysandstthomas.nhs.uk (pages 68–9)

Handel House Museum, 25 Brook Street, London, W1K 4HB.
www.handelhouse.org (pages 22, 25–8)

Harewood House, Harewood, Leeds, West Yorkshire, LS17 9LG.
www.harewood.org (page 32)

Hogarth's House, Hogarth Lane, Chiswick, London W4 2QN.

www.hounslow.info/arts/hogarthshouse
Built around 1700, this was Hogarth's country home from 1749 until
his death in 1764.

The House of St Barnabas, 1 Greek Street, London, W1D 3NQ.
www.hosb.org.uk
Richard Beckford's house. (pages 25, 26)

Museum of London, 150 London Wall, London, EC2Y 5HN.
www.museumoflondon.org.uk

Museum of the Royal College of Surgeons of England, 35–43 Lincoln's Inn
Fields, London, WC2A 3PE. www.rcseng.ac.uk
At the core of the museum's displays is the extraordinary collection of
the famous surgeon John Hunter (pages 18, 29, 74, 75, 77).

National Maritime Museum, Romney Road, Greenwich, London, SE10 9NF.
www.nmm.ac.uk

National Army Museum, Royal Hospital Road, Chelsea, London, SW3 4HT,
www.national-army-museum.ac.uk

No.1 Royal Crescent, Bath, Avon, BA1, 2LR.
www.bath-preservation-trust.org.uk

The Royal Hospital Chelsea, Royal Hospital Road, London, SW3 4SR.
www.chelsea-pensioners.co.uk
Designed by Sir Christopher Wren and completed in 1692 this is still
the home of the Chelsea Pensioners (army veterans).

St Bartholomew's Hospital, West Smithfield, London, EC1A 7BE.
www.bartsandthelondon.nhs.uk

St Paul's Church, Covent Garden, Bedford Street, London, WC2E 9ED.
www.actorschurch.org
One of the last remnants of the original Inigo Jones Piazza and in the
heart of theatreland, St Paul's is known as the Actors' Church. (page 36)

The Seven Stars, 53 Carey Street, WC2A 7JB. (page 42)

Sir John Soane's Museum, 13 Lincoln's Inn Fields, London, WC2A 3BP.
www.soane.org
The former home of architect Sir John Soane, the collection includes
Hogarth's *A Rake's Progress* (page 11) and The Election Series.

Tate Britain, Millbank, London, SW1P 4RG. www.tate.org.uk/britain
The home of British Art from 1500 to the present.

Tunbridge Wells Museum & Art Gallery, Civic Centre, Mount Pleasant, Royal
Tunbridge Wells, Kent, TN1 1JN.
www.tunbridgewellsmuseum.org

The British Galleries & Costume Collection, Victoria and Albert Museum,
Cromwell Road, London, SW7 2RL. www.vam.ac.uk
British art and design from the reign of Henry VIII to Victoria.

Ye Olde Cheshire Cheese, 145 Fleet Street, London, EC4A 2BU. (page 41)

INDEX

Page numbers in italic refer to illustrations